ALASKA

PHOTOGRAPHS BY ELIZABETH KRAMER

THIS IS PART OF THE VISITING SERIES.

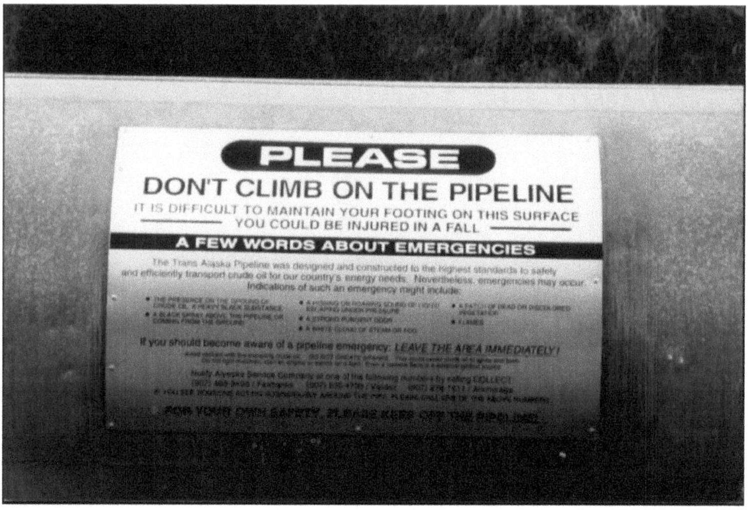
PLEASE
DON'T CLIMB ON THE PIPELINE
IT IS DIFFICULT TO MAINTAIN YOUR FOOTING ON THIS SURFACE
YOU COULD BE INJURED IN A FALL
A FEW WORDS ABOUT EMERGENCIES
The Trans Alaska Pipeline was designed and constructed to the highest standards to safely and efficiently transport crude oil for our country's energy needs. Nevertheless, emergencies may occur. Indications of such an emergency might include:
If you should become aware of a pipeline emergency: LEAVE THE AREA IMMEDIATELY!

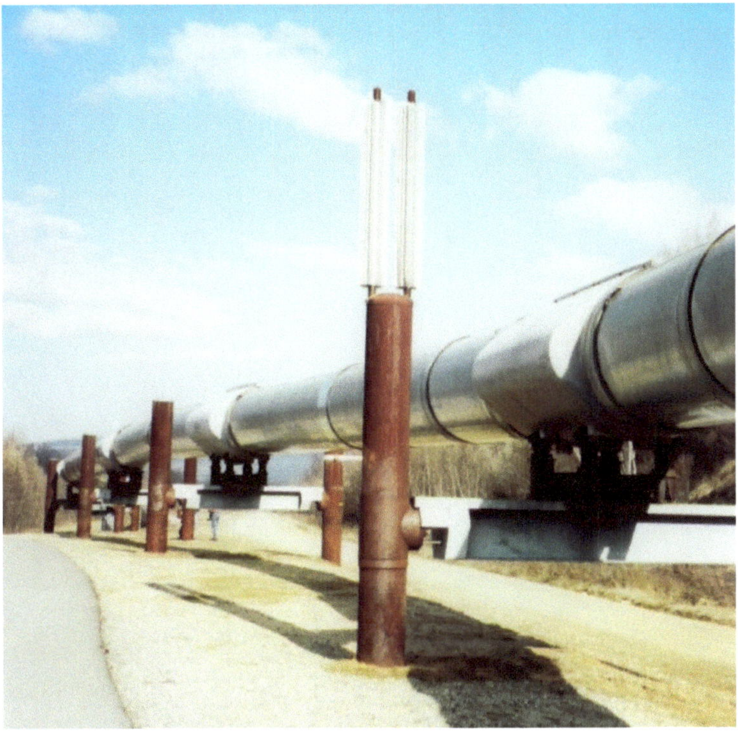

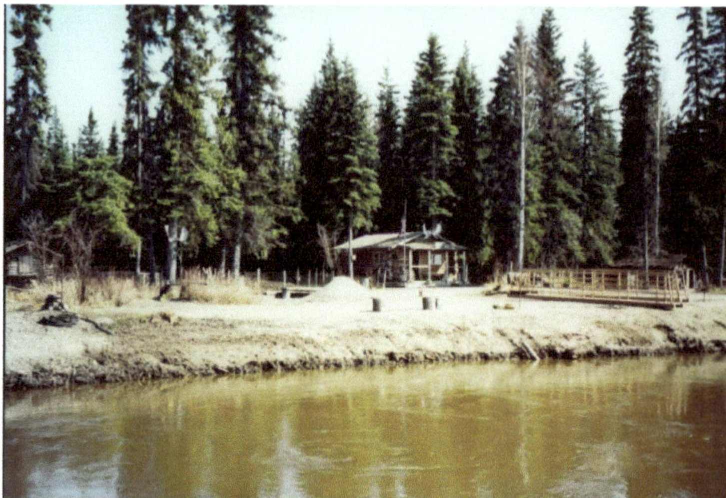

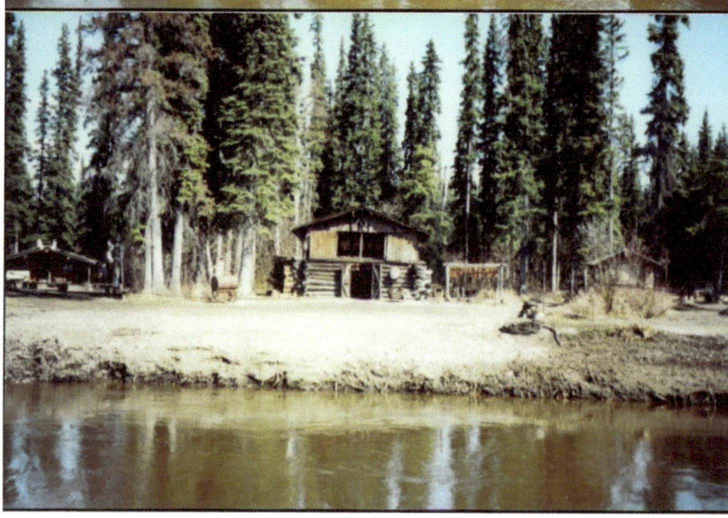

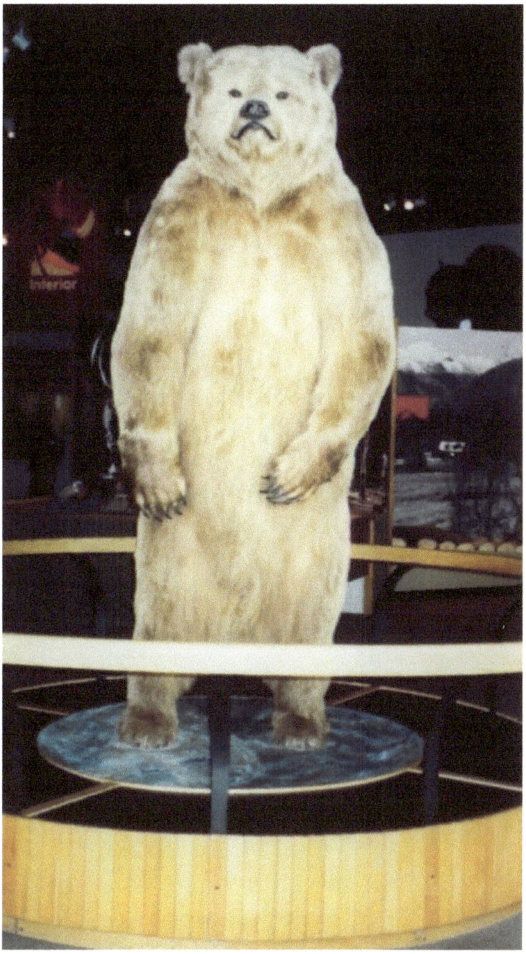
Interior

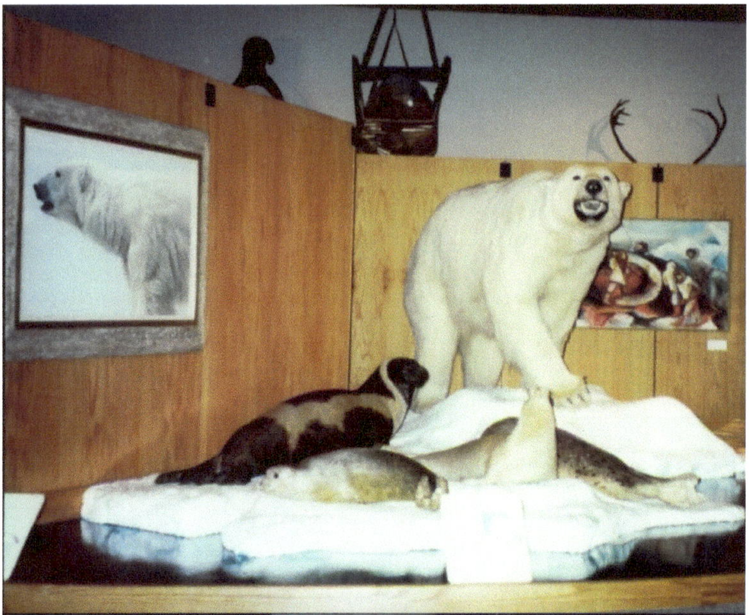

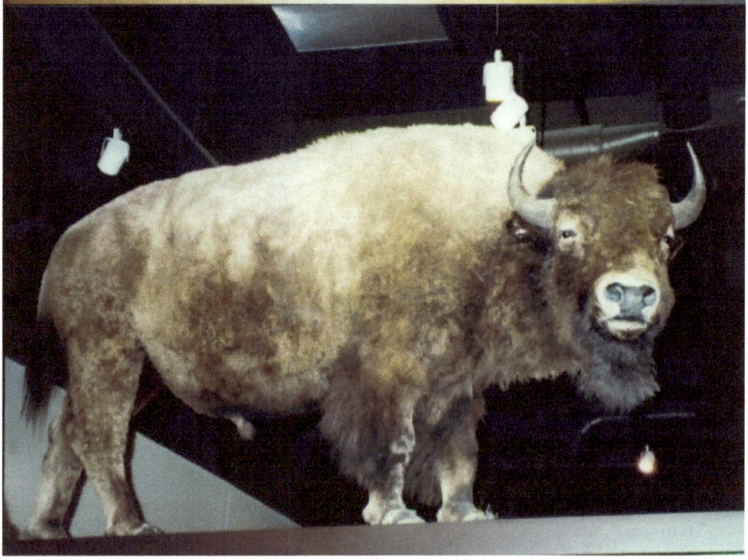

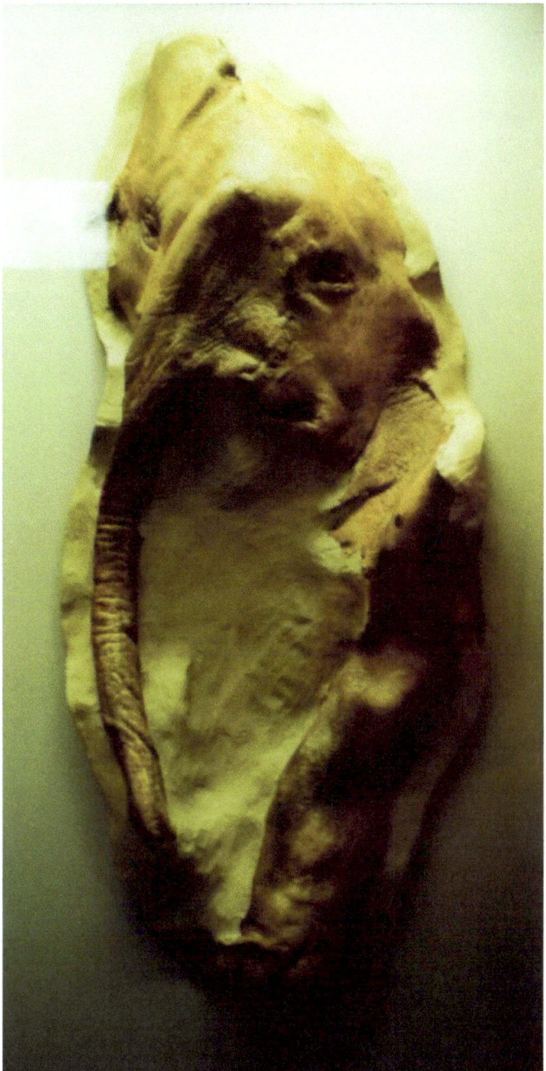

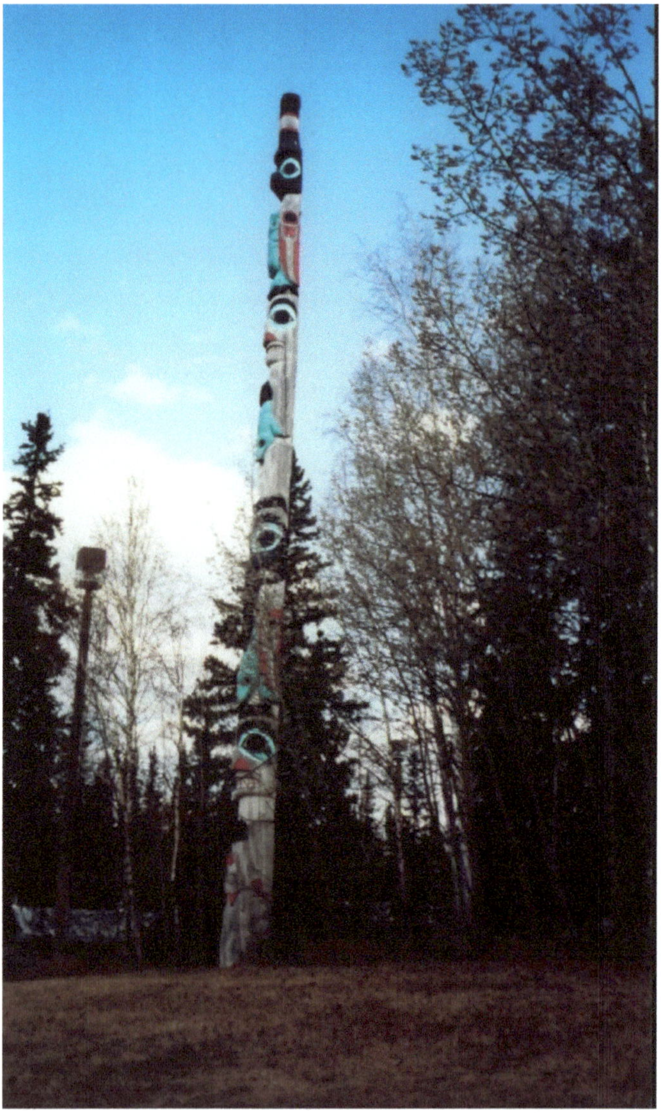

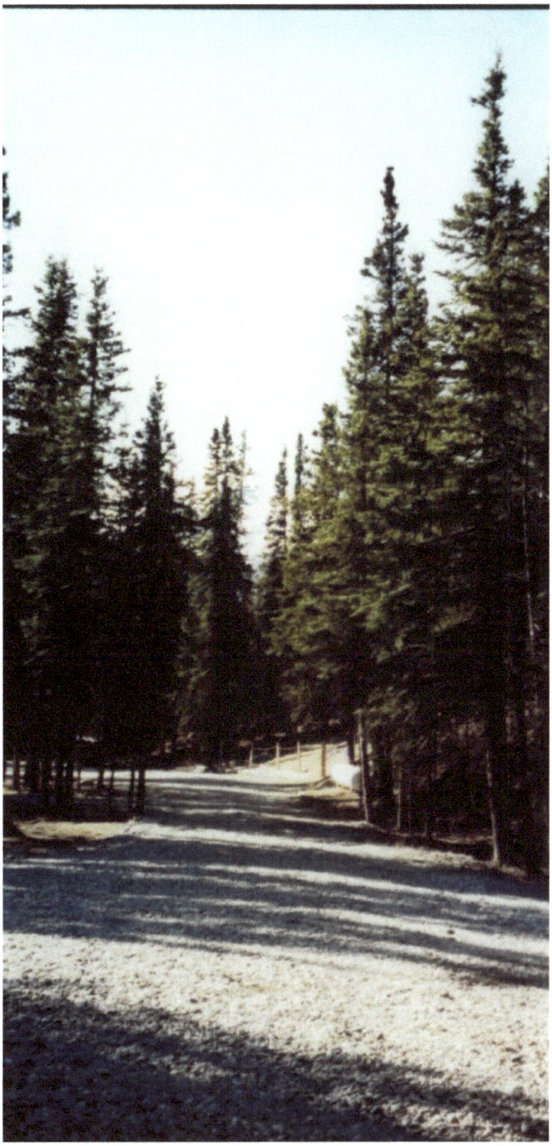

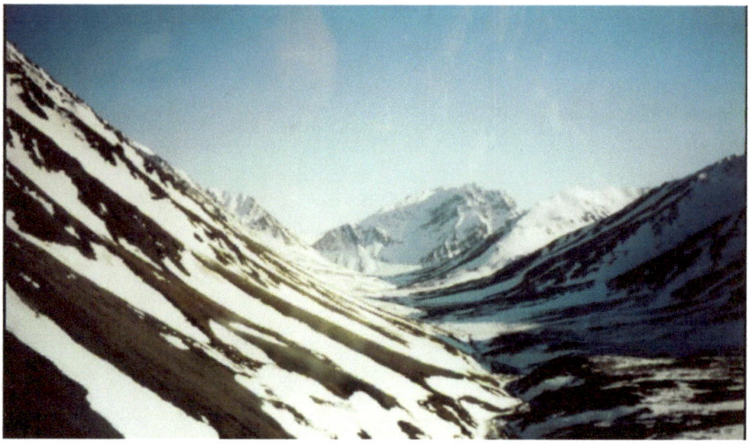

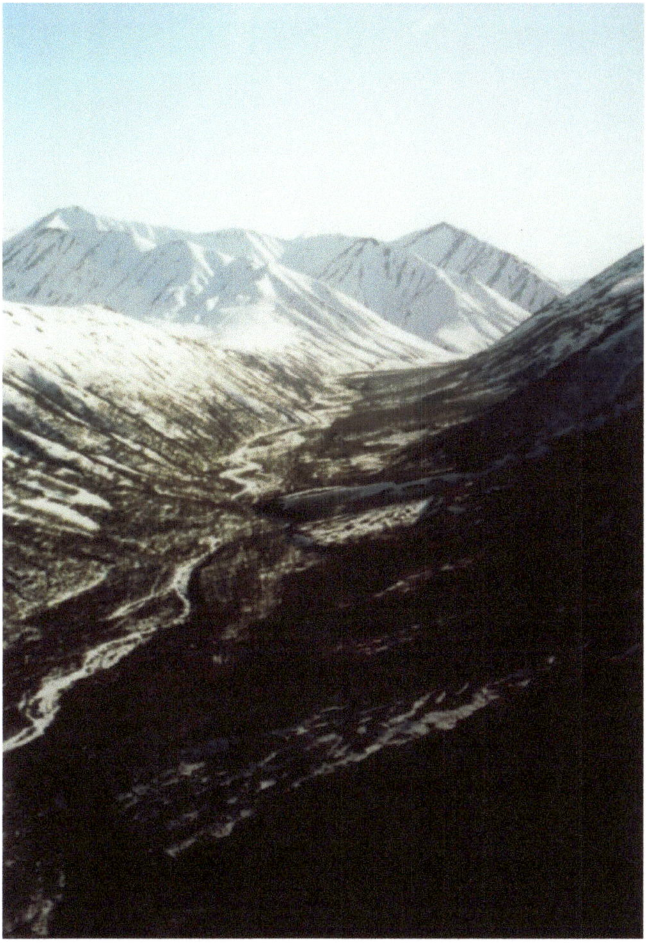

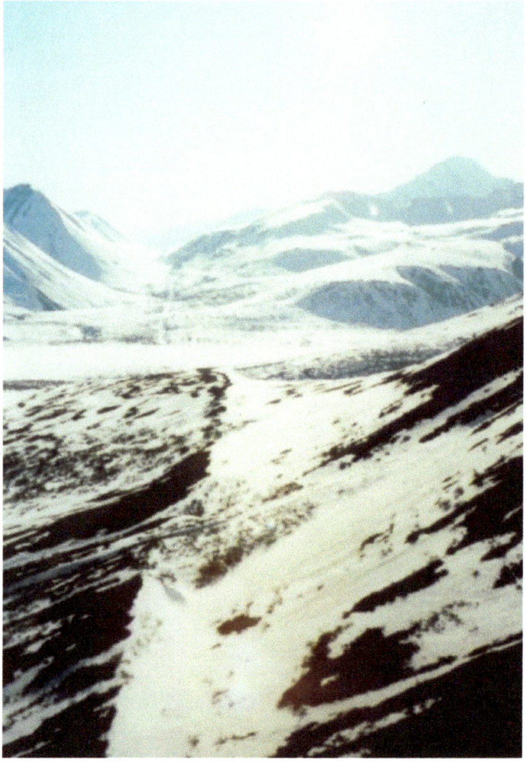

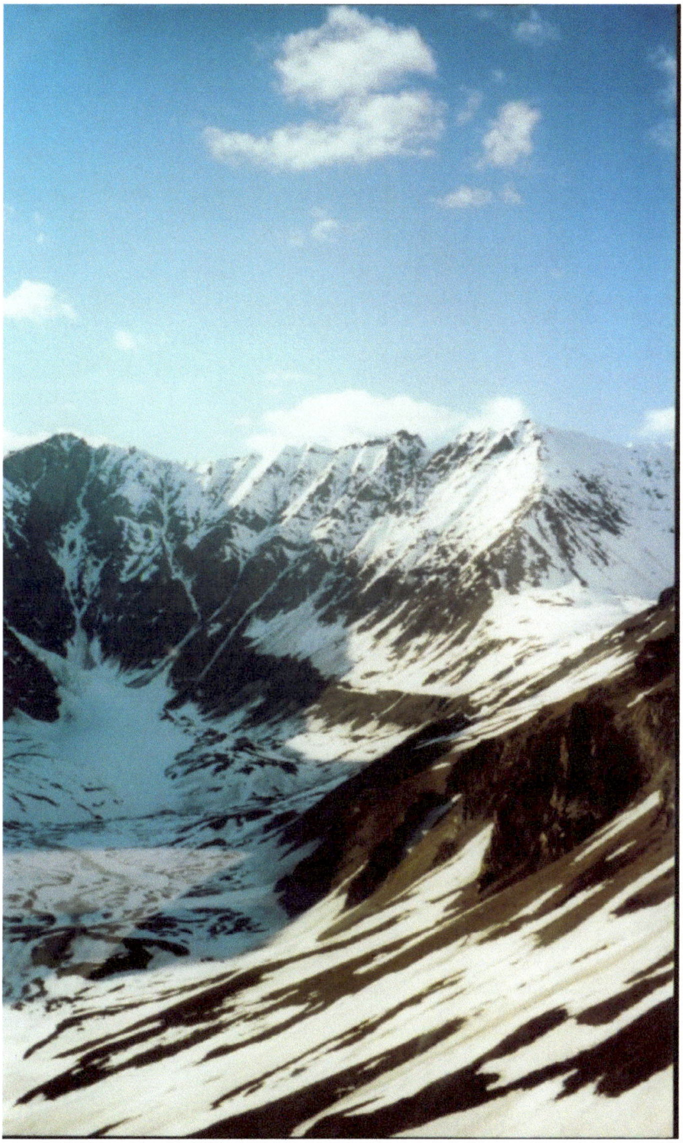

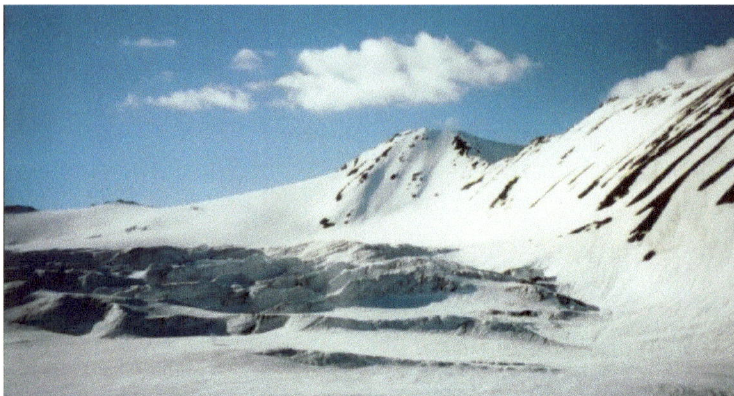

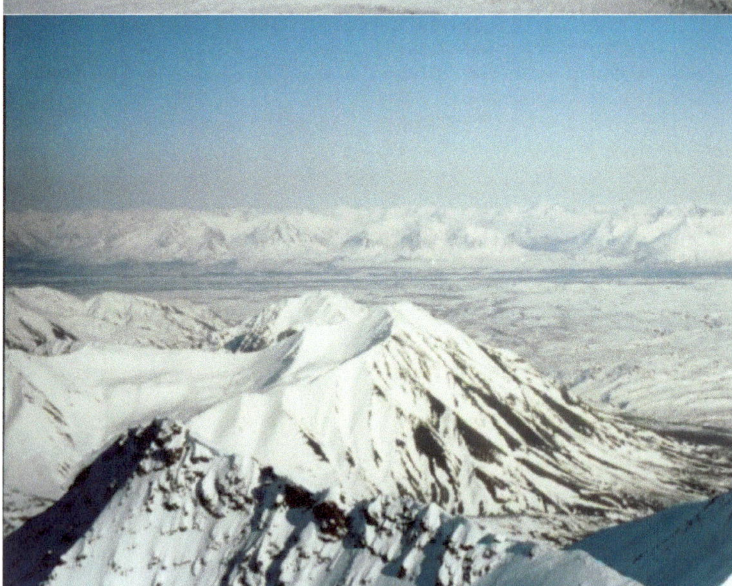

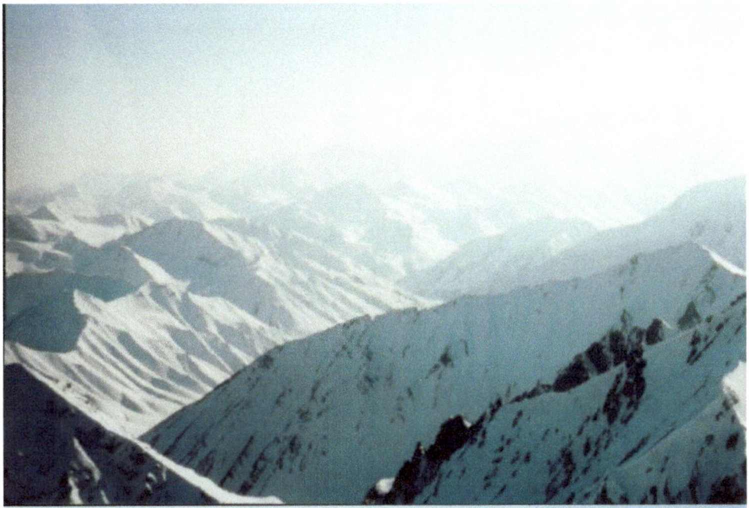

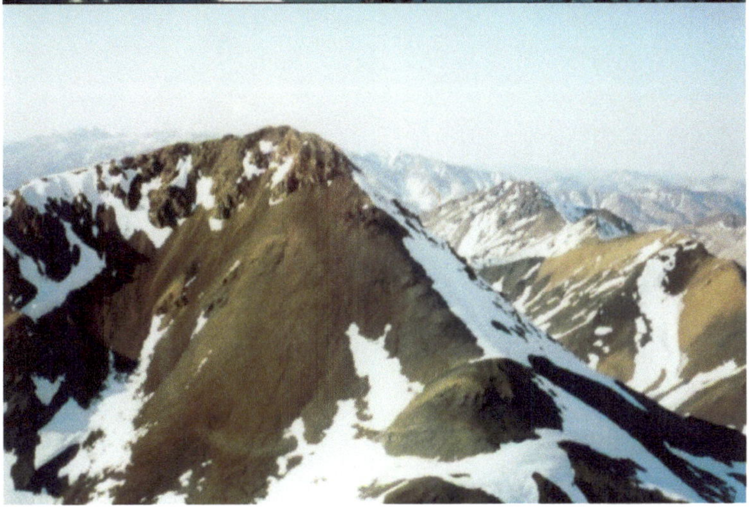

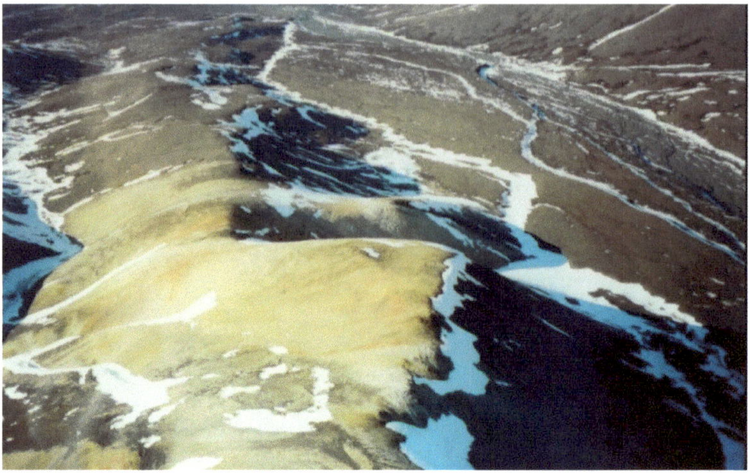

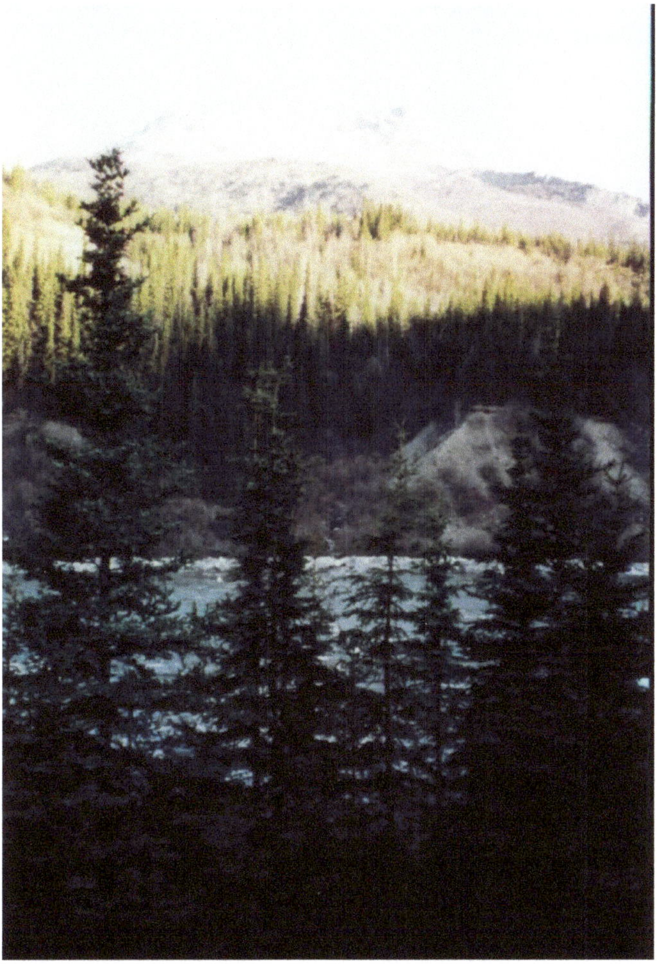

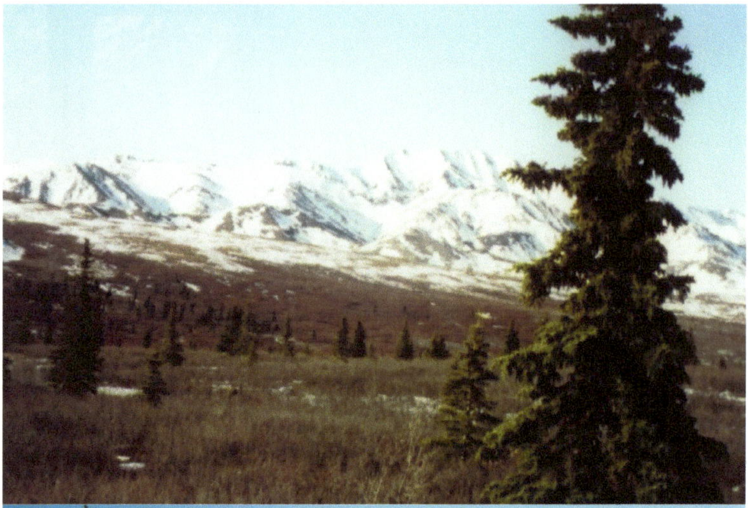

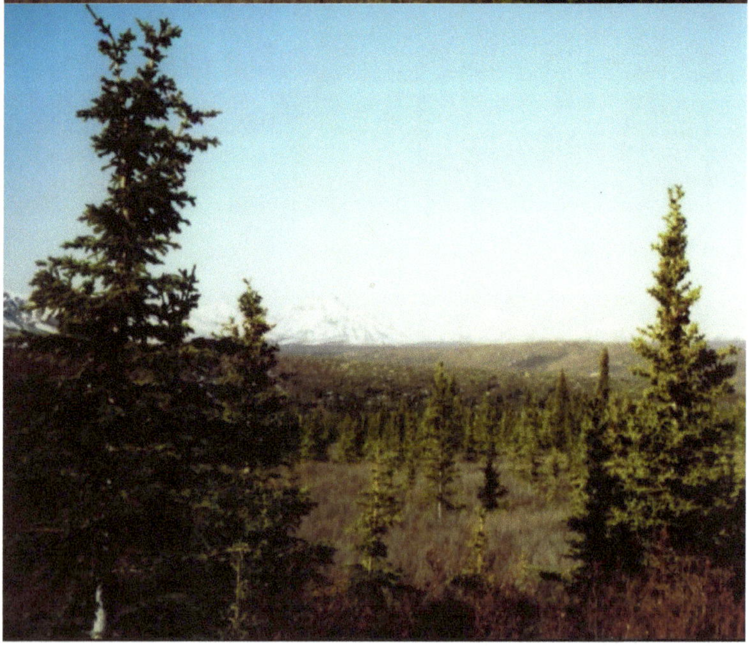

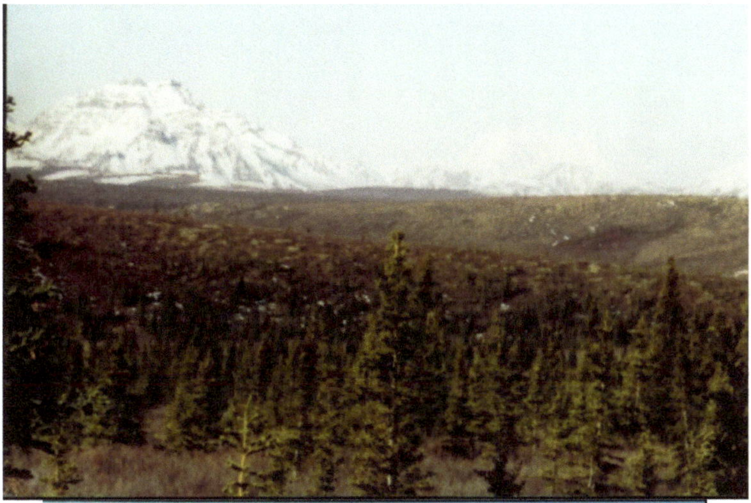

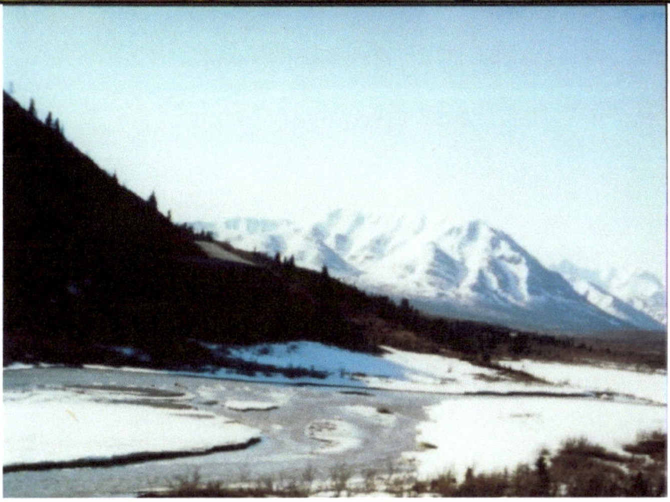

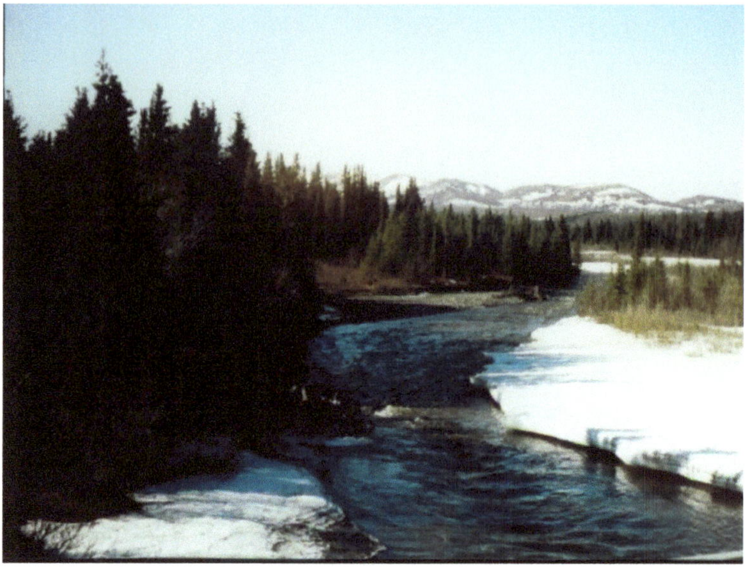

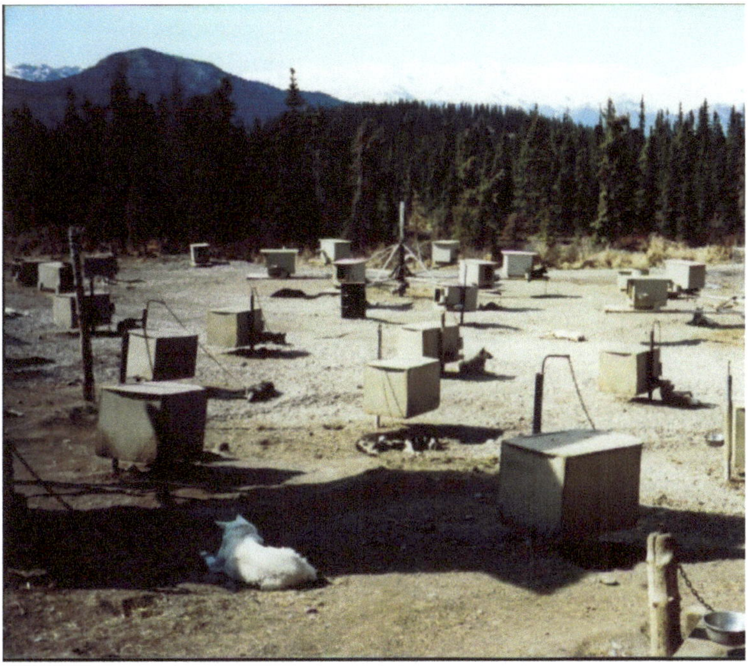

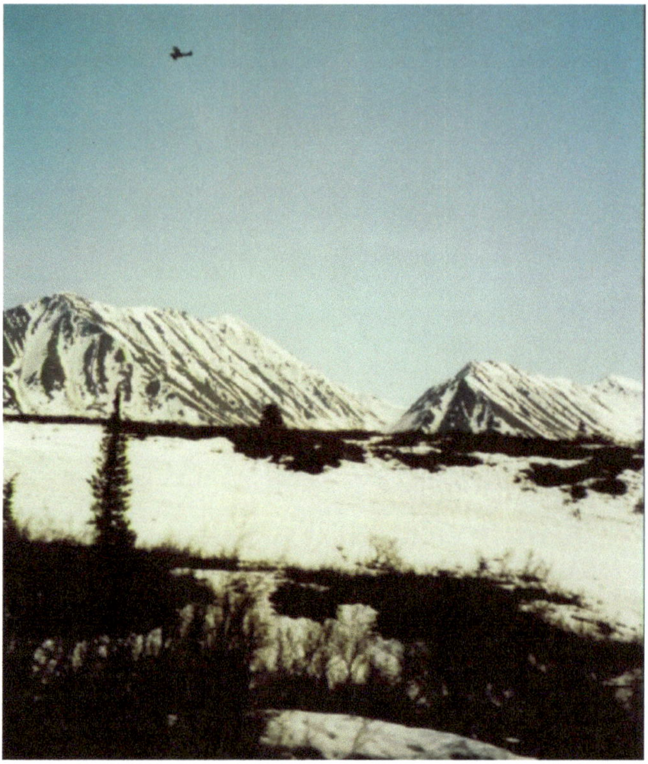

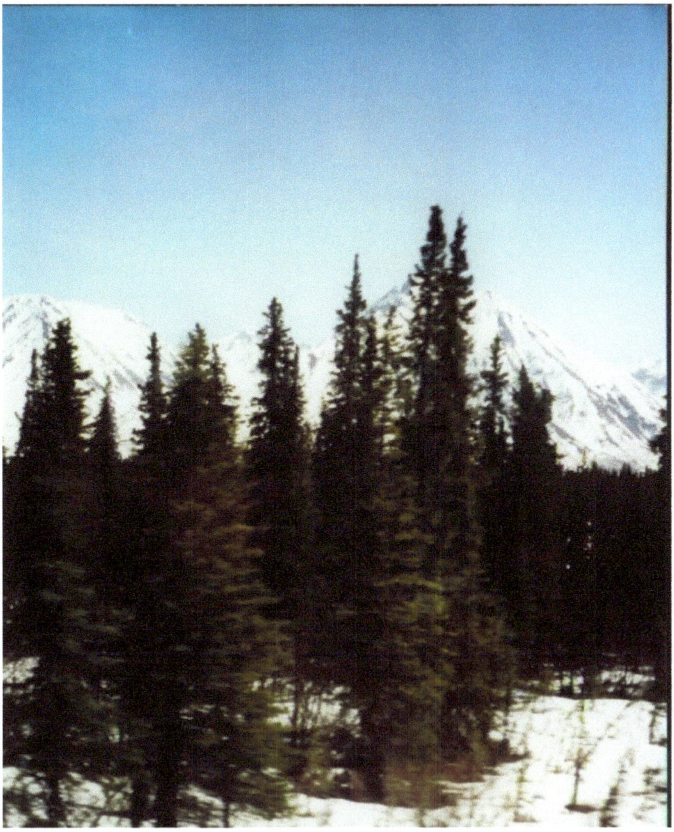

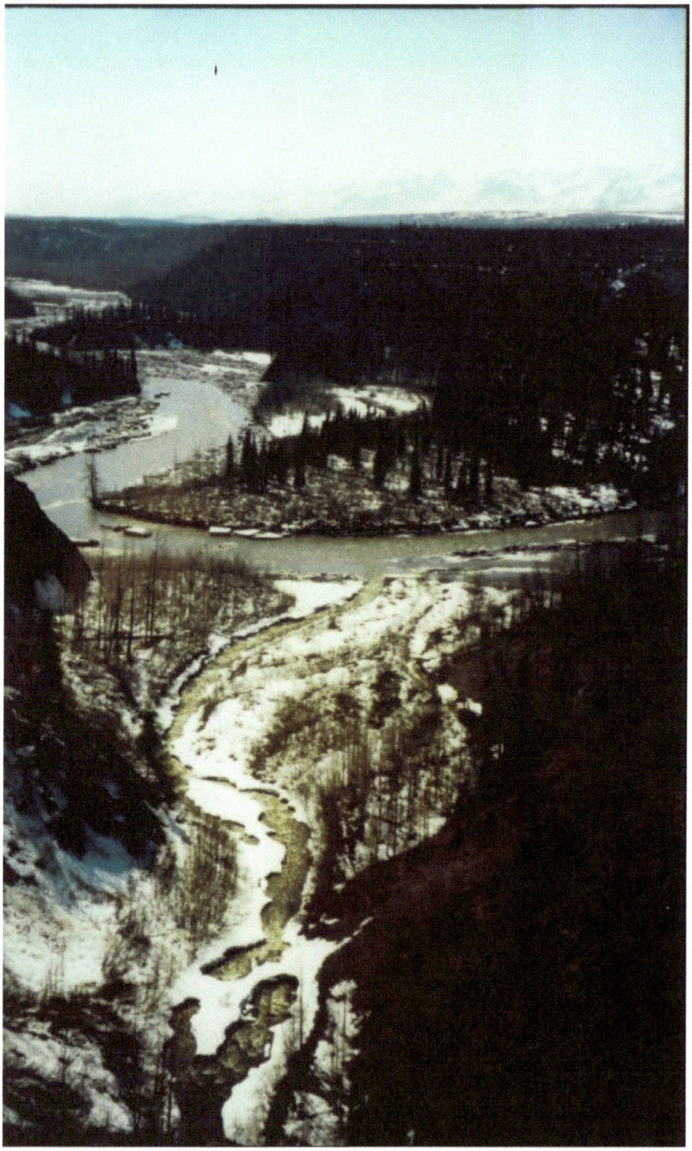

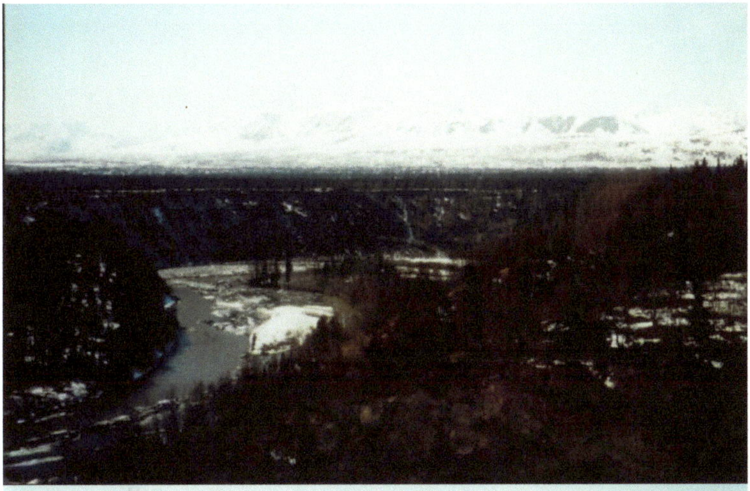

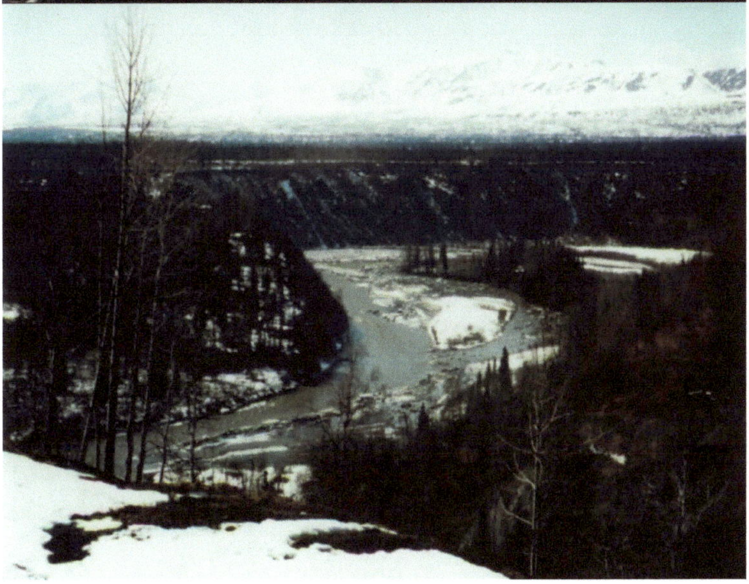

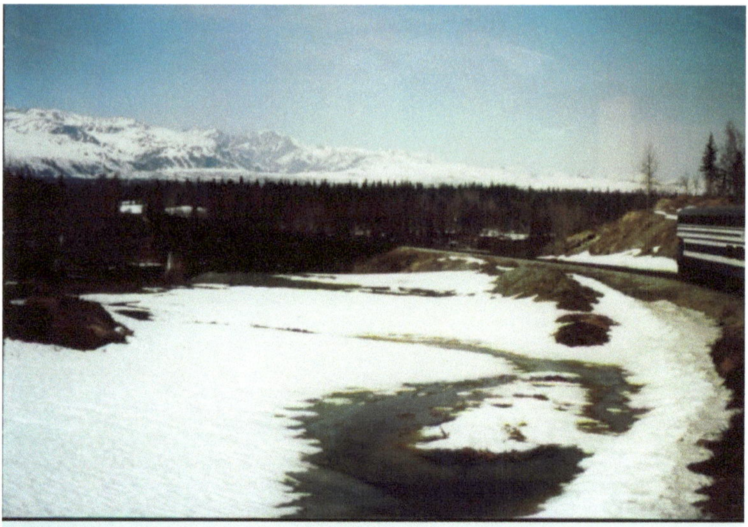
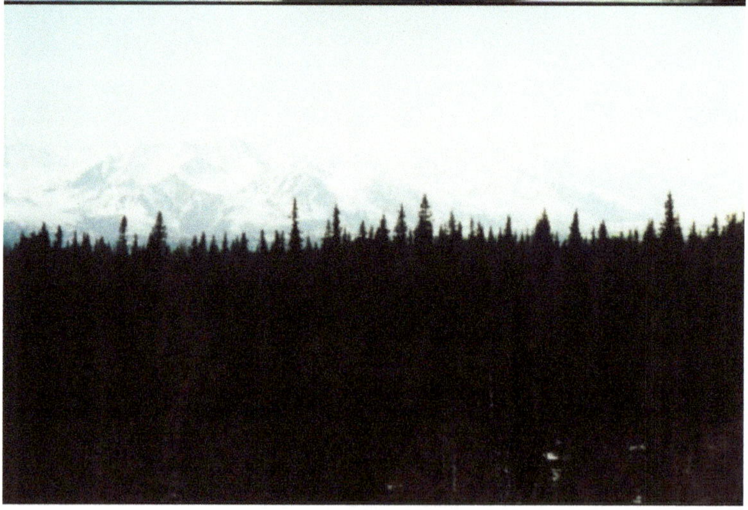

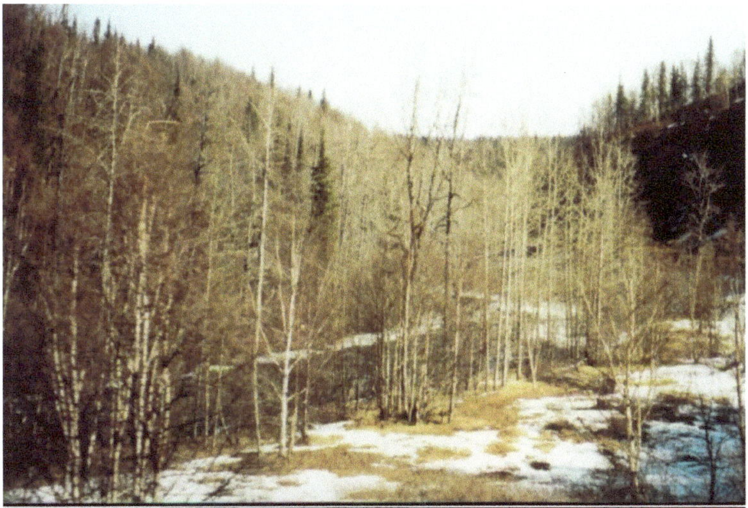

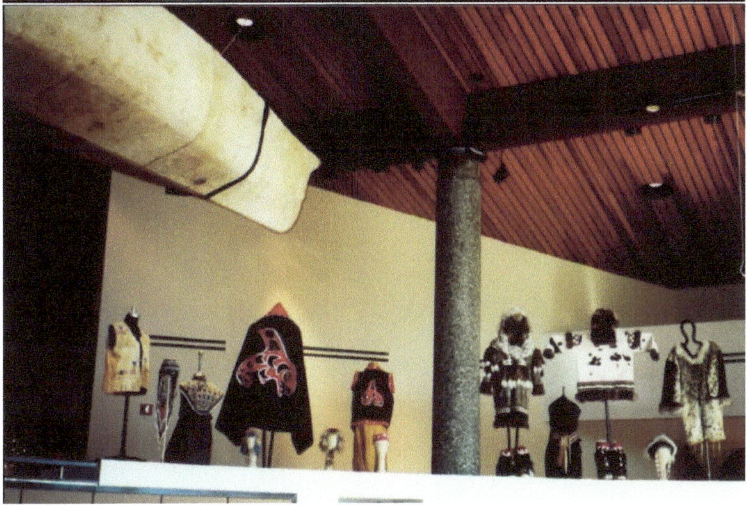

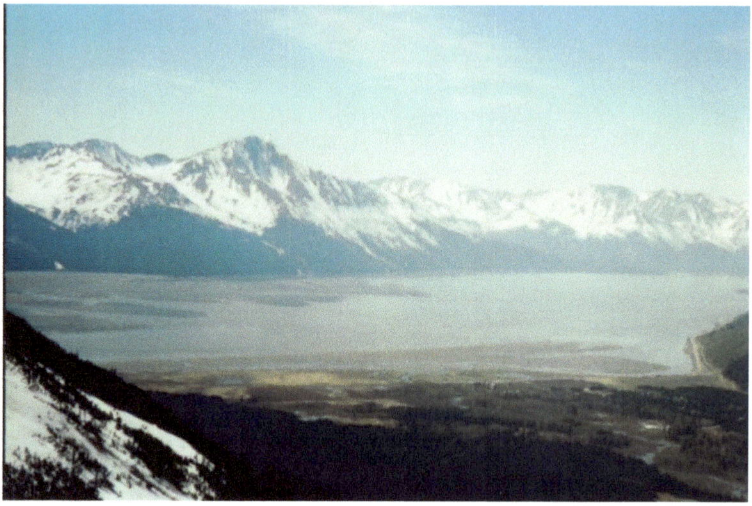

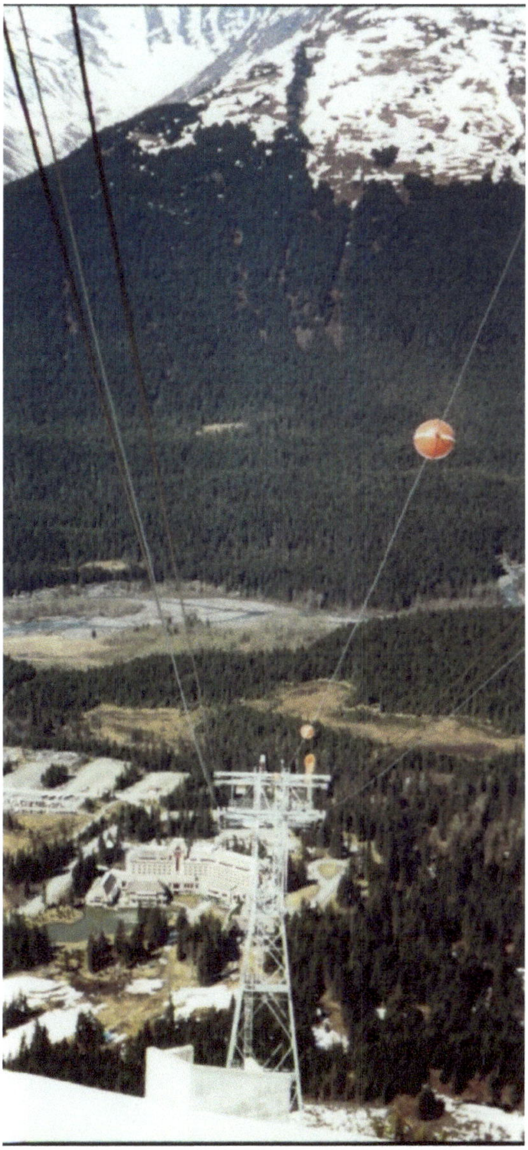

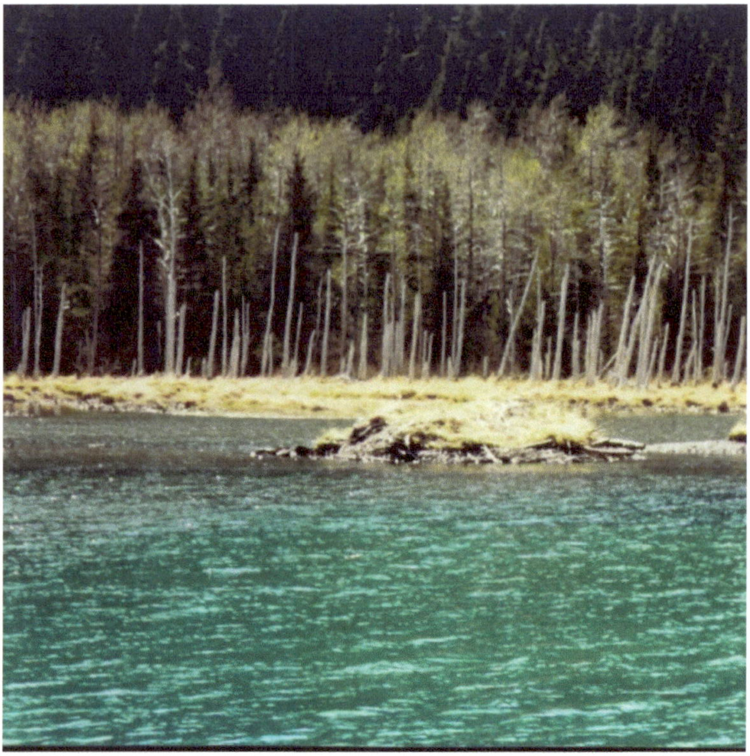

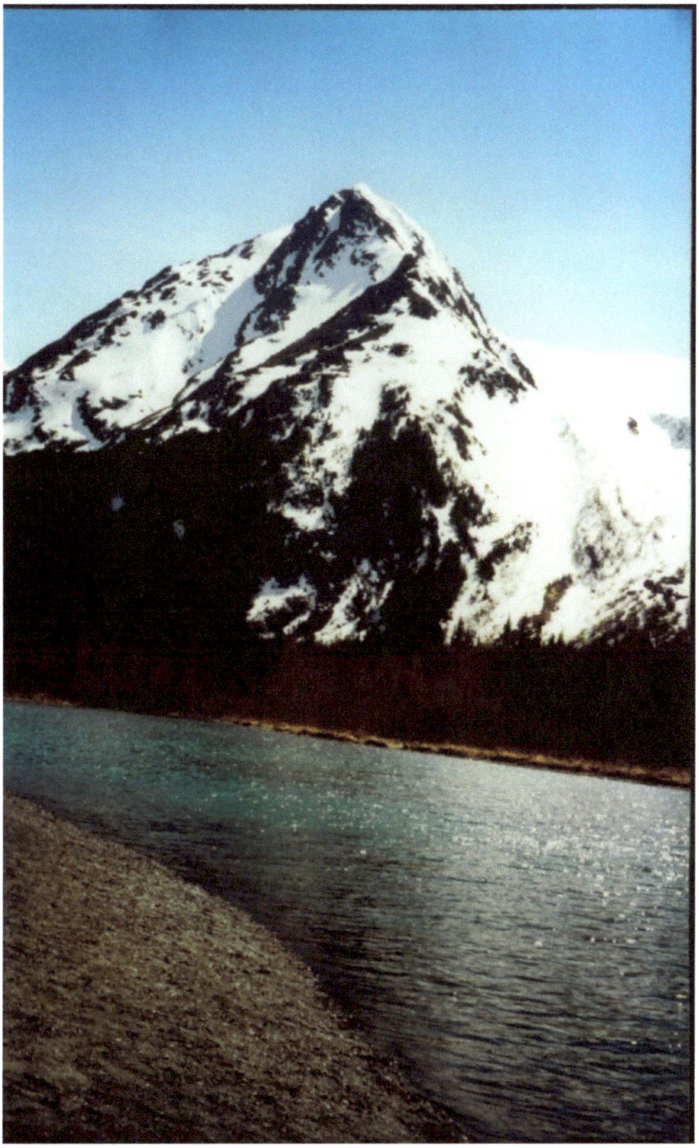

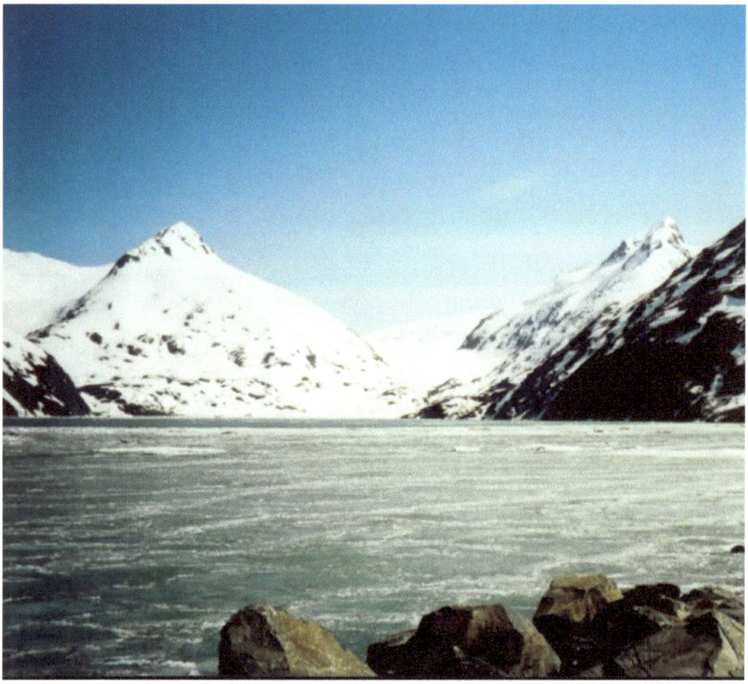

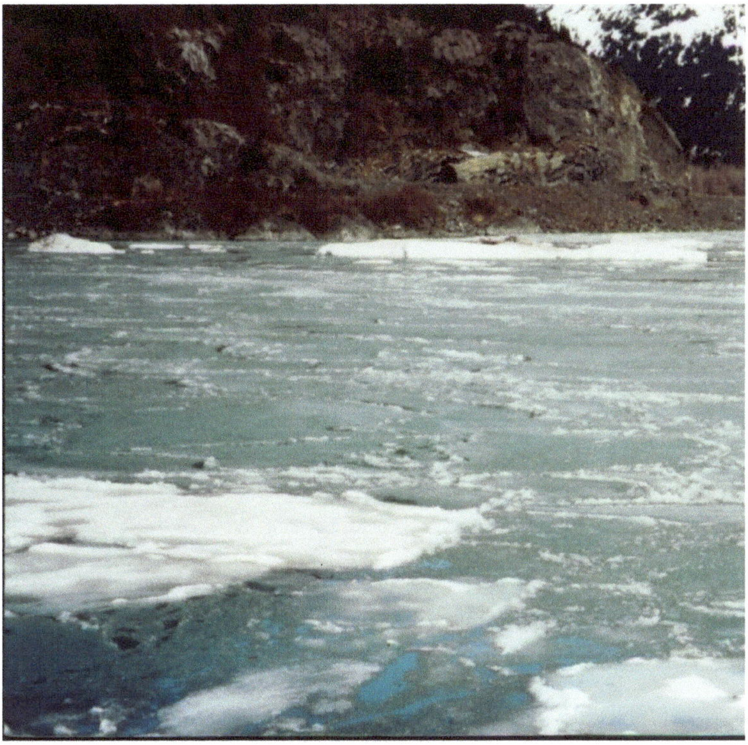

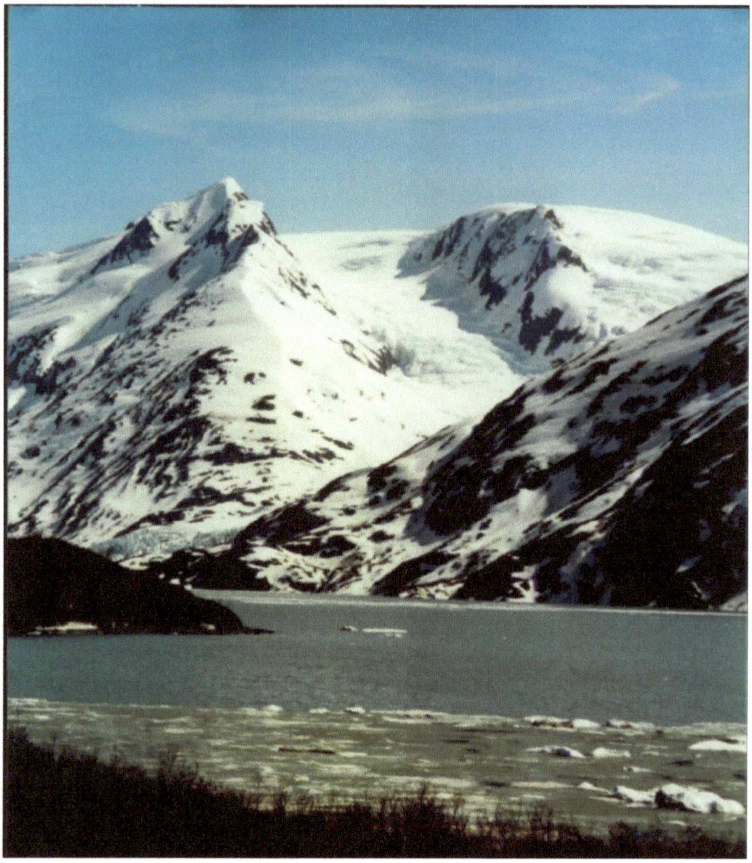

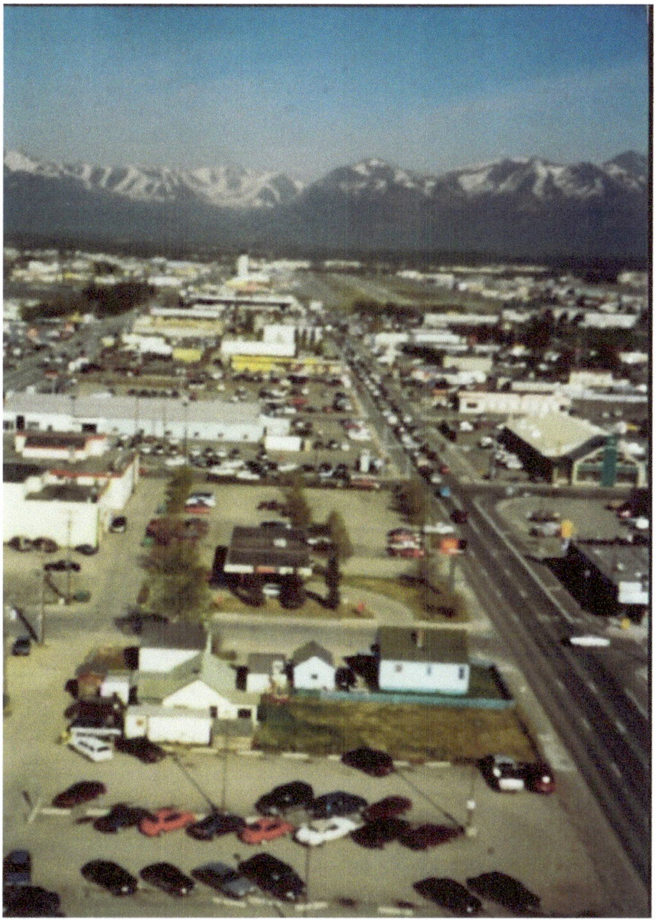

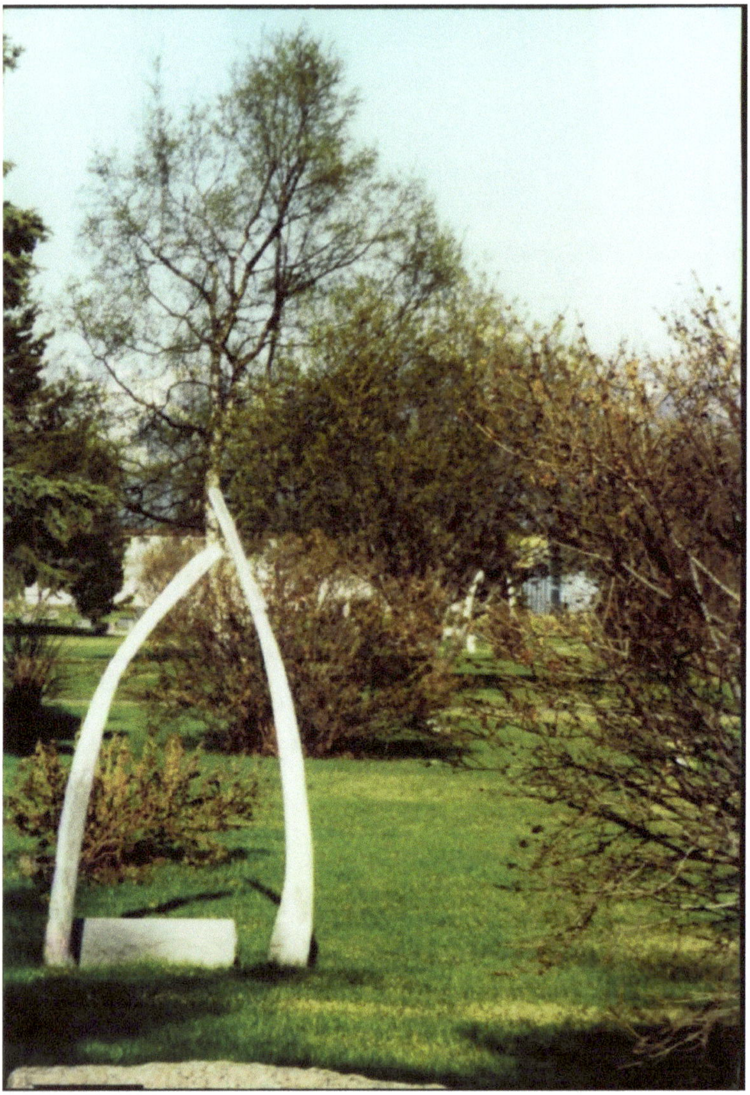

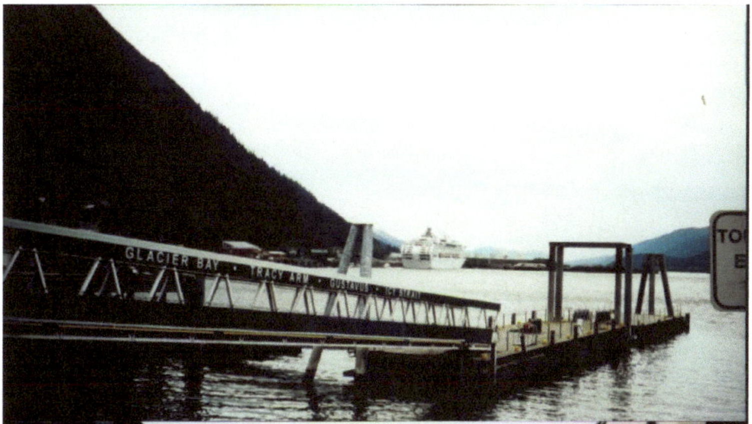
GLACIER BAY · TRACY ARM · GUSTAVUS
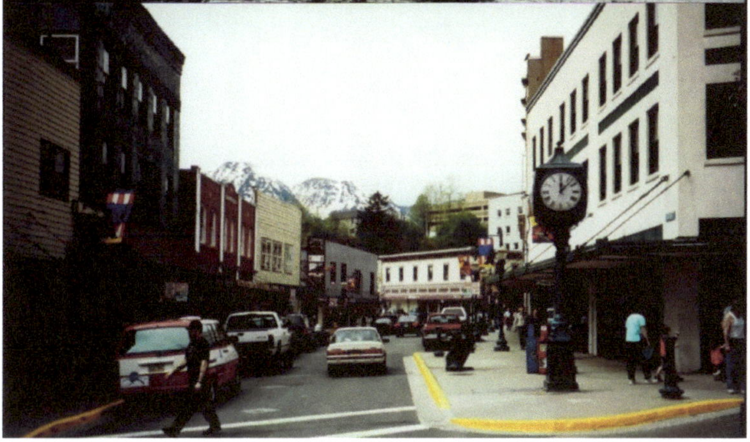

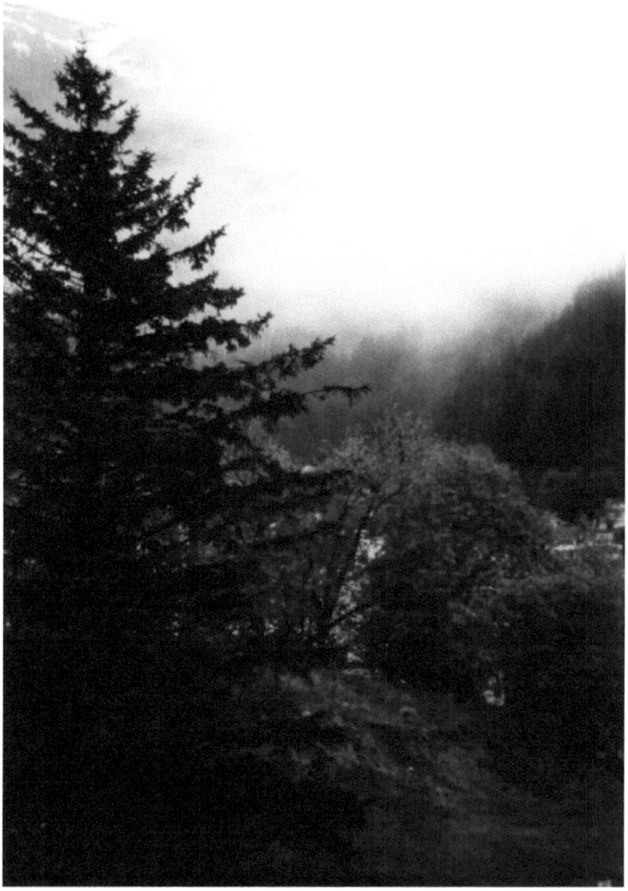

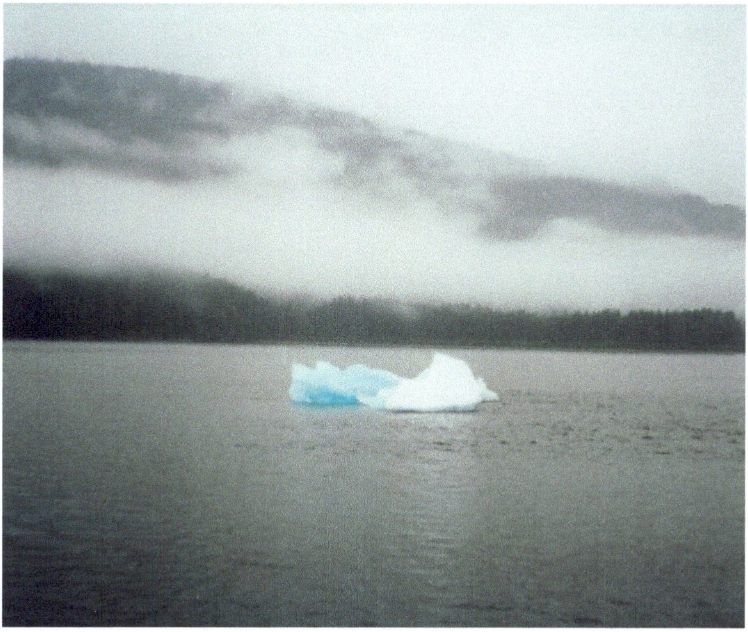

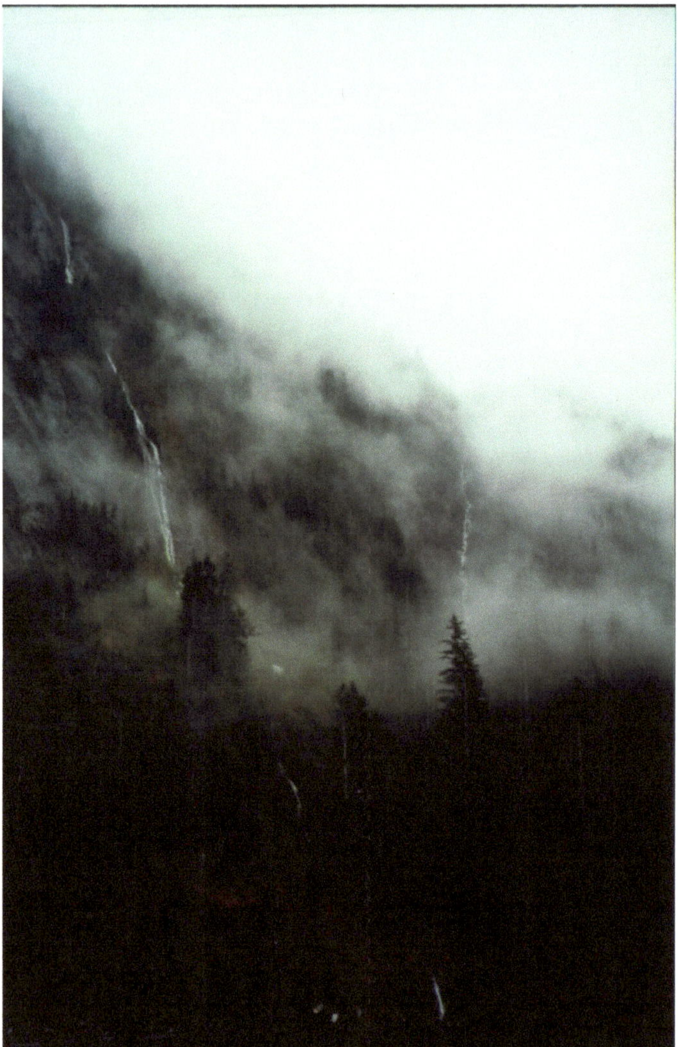

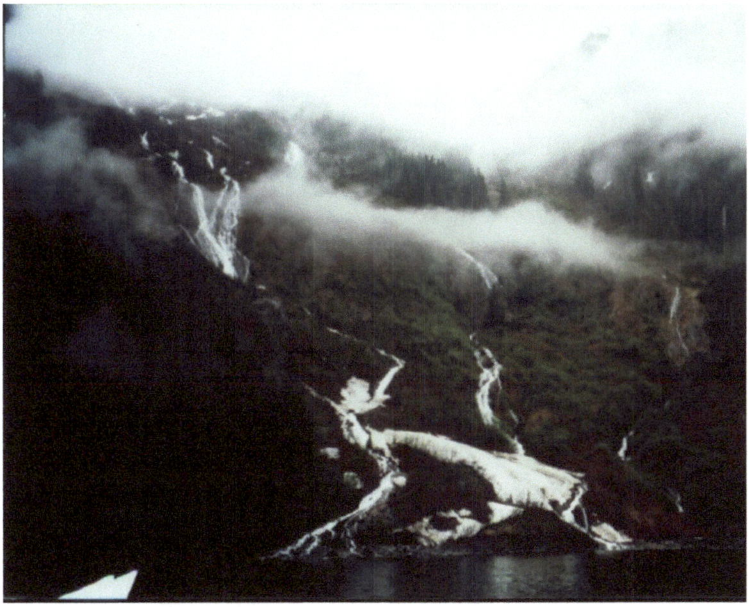

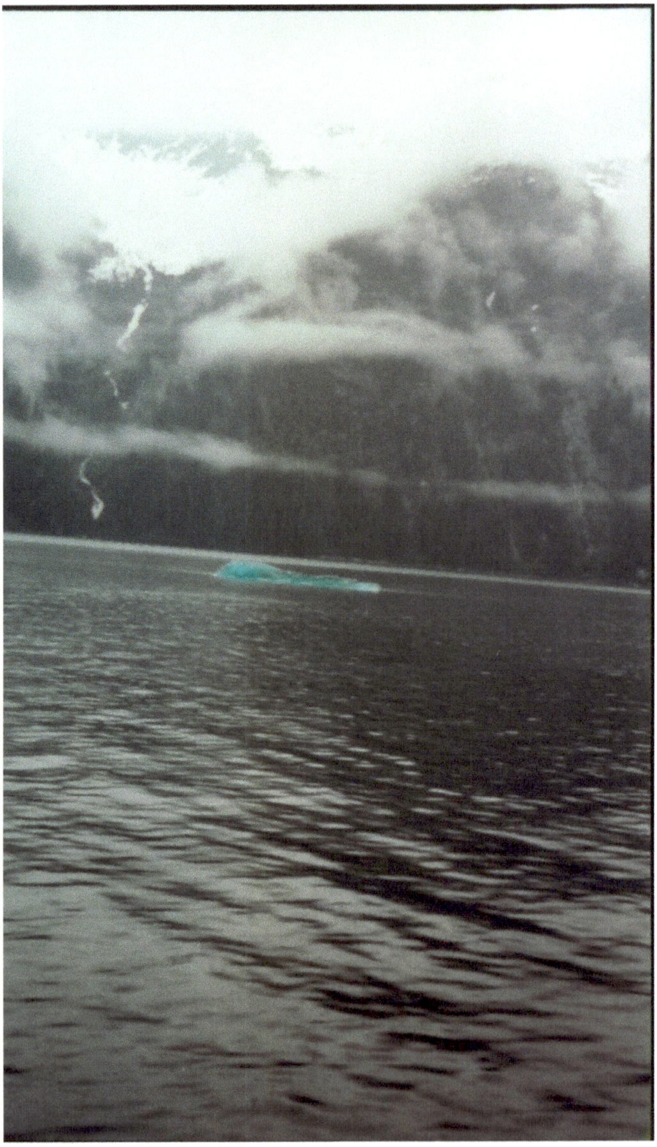

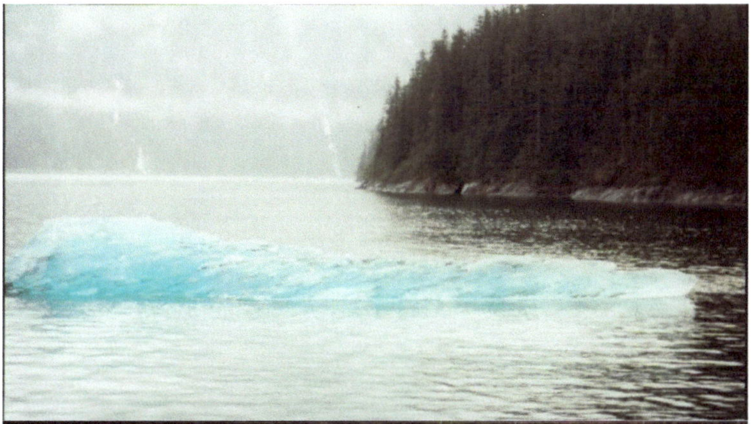
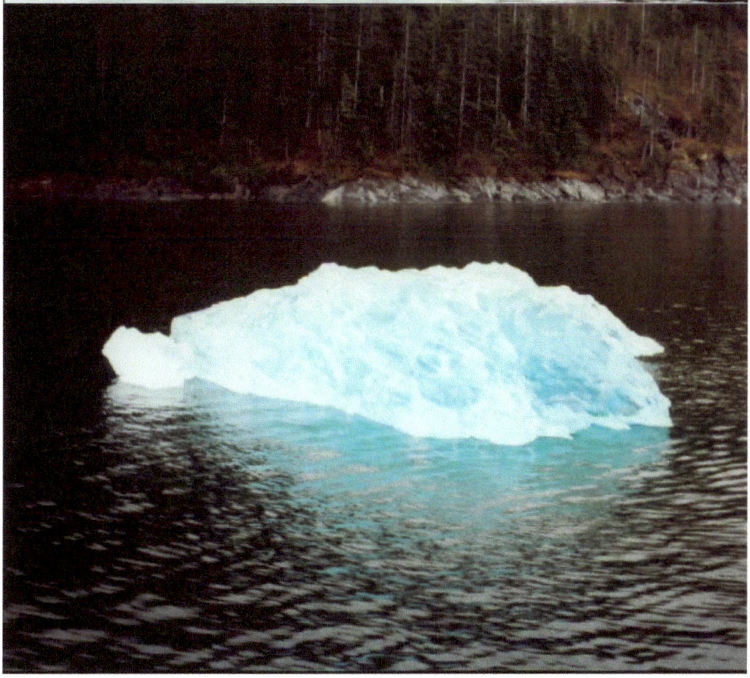

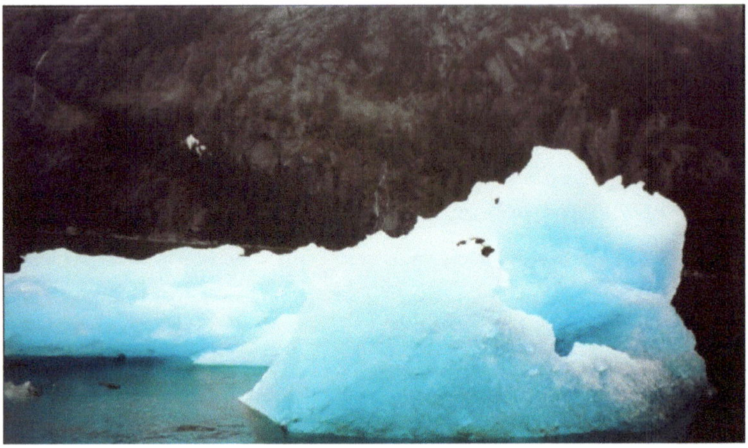

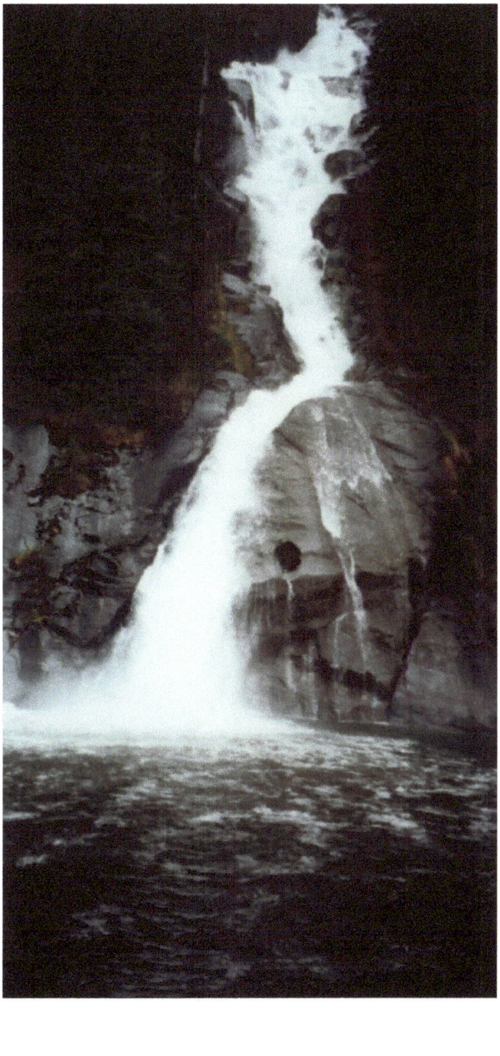

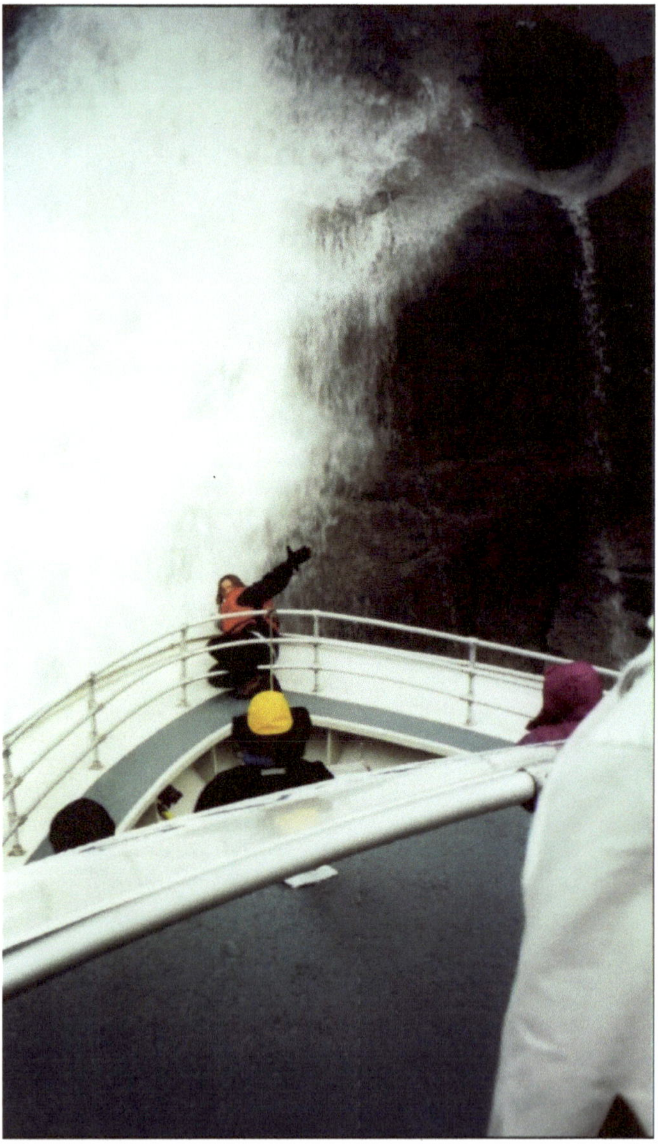

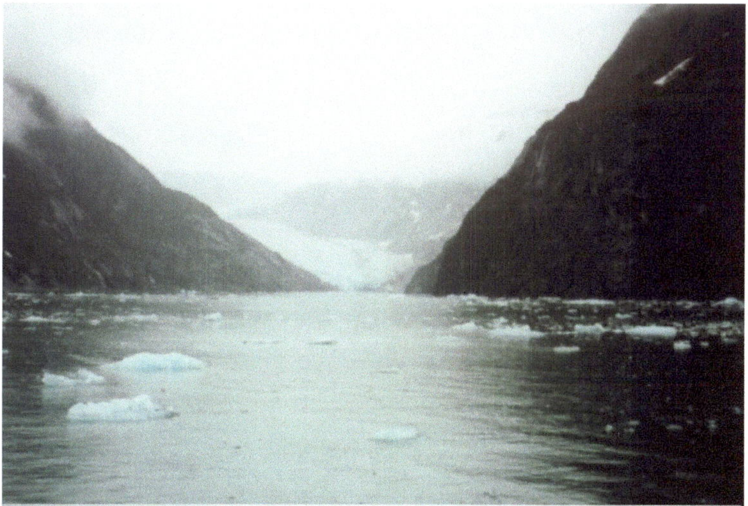

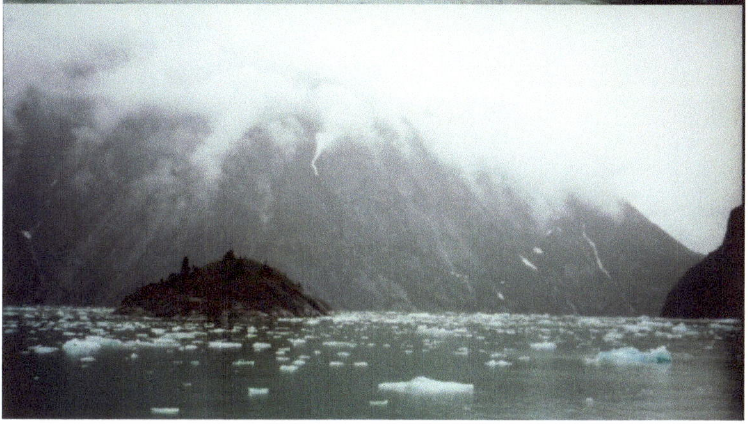

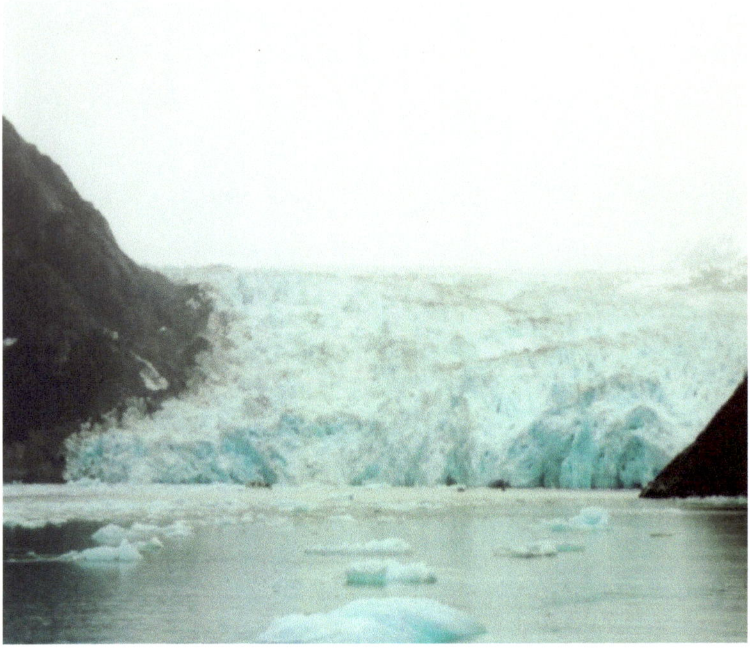

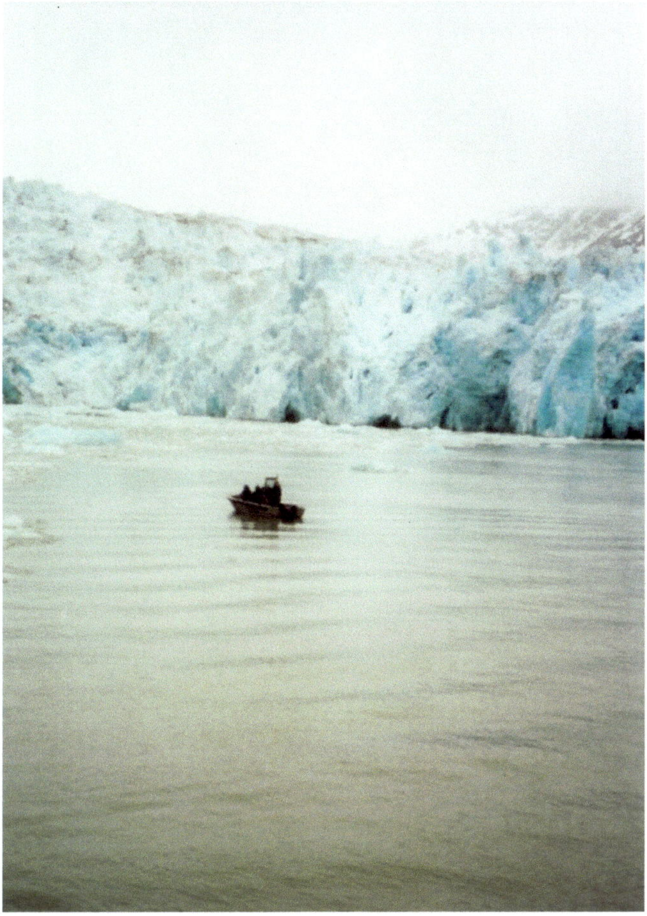

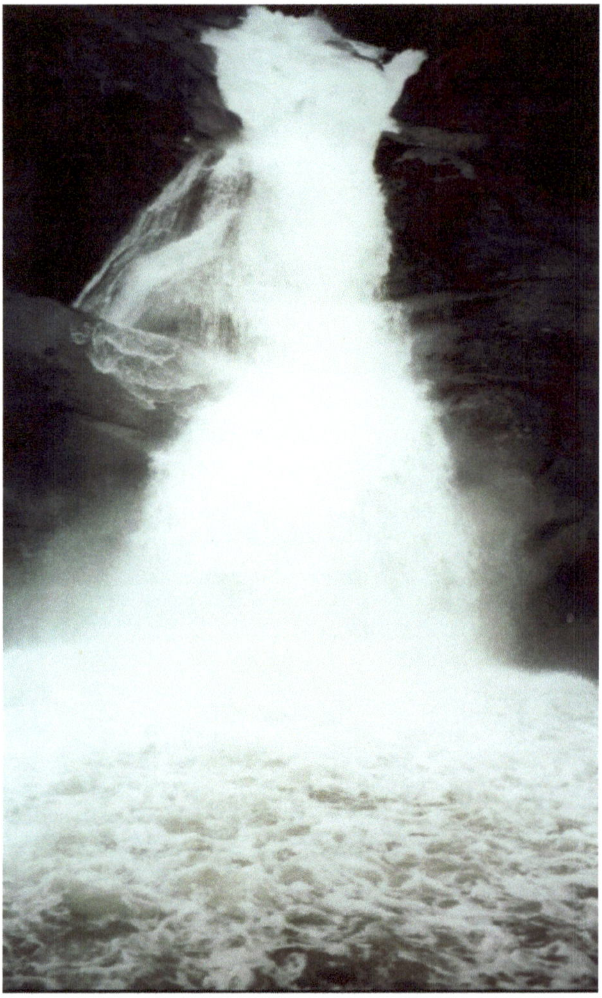

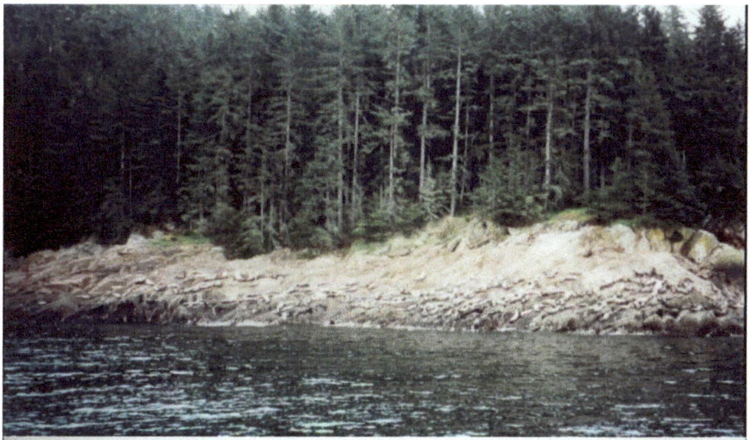
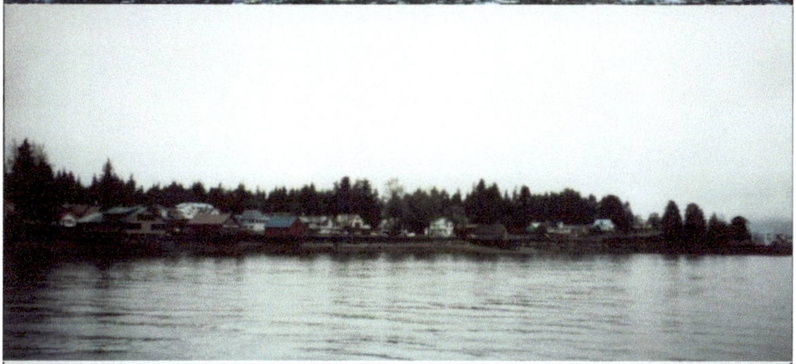
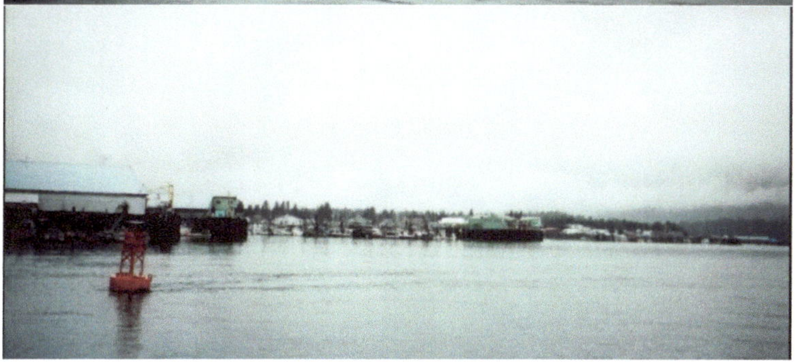

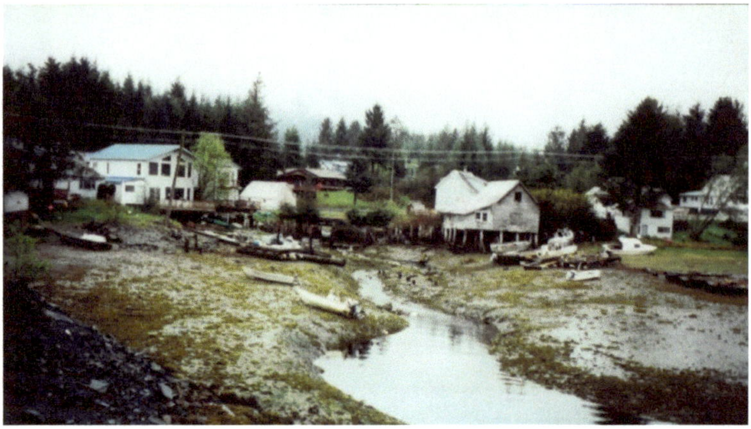

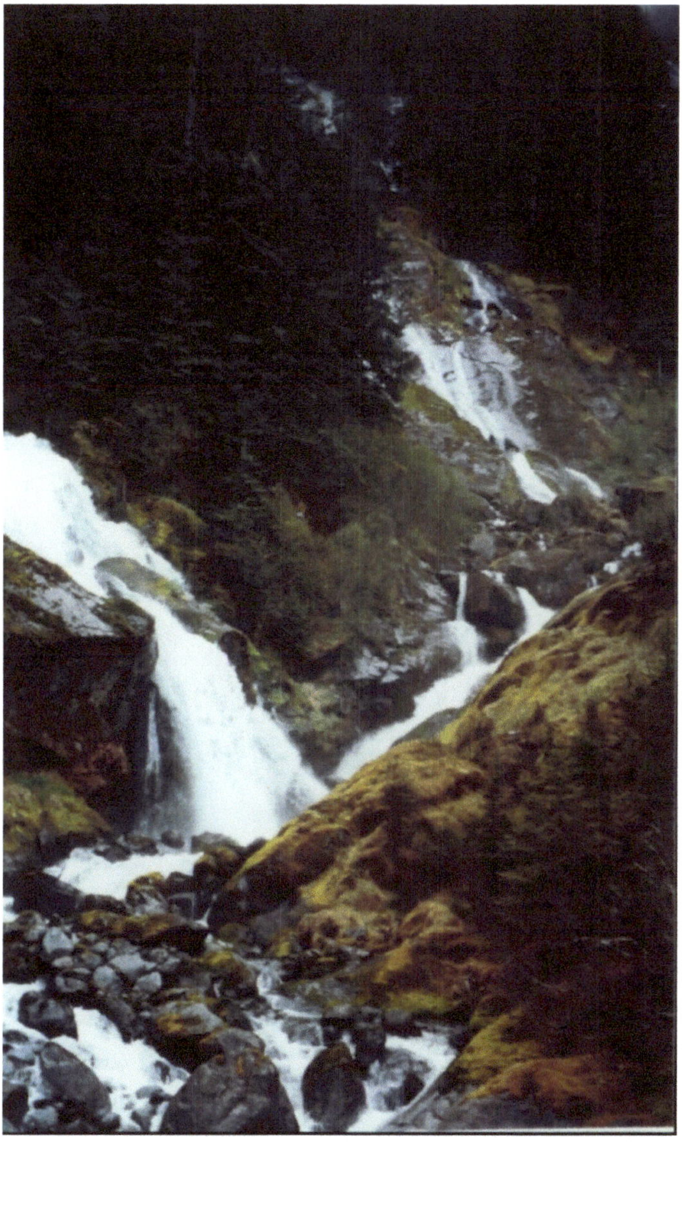

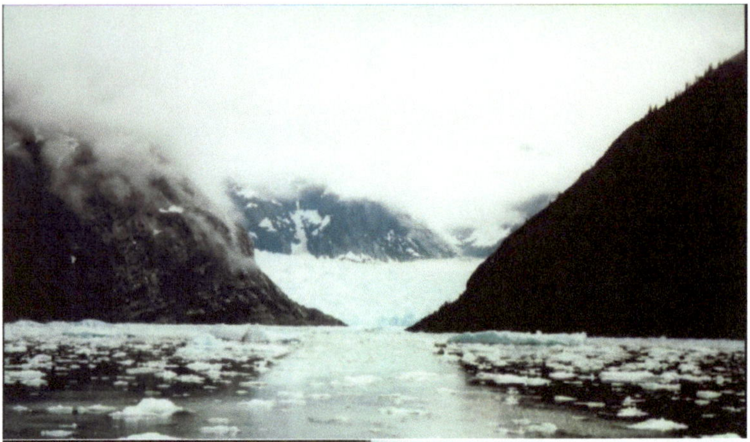

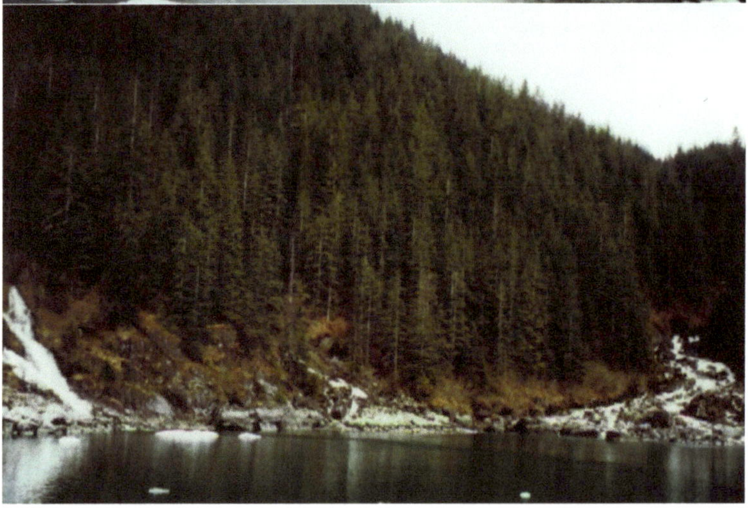

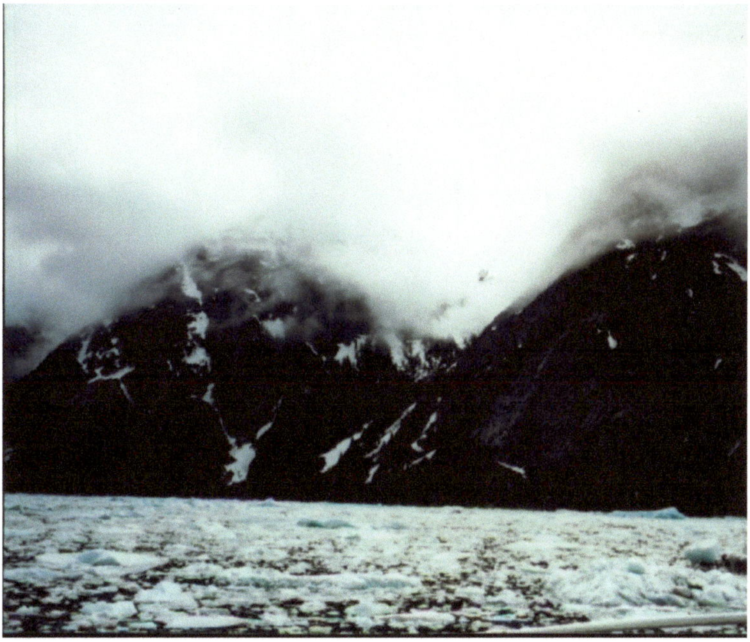

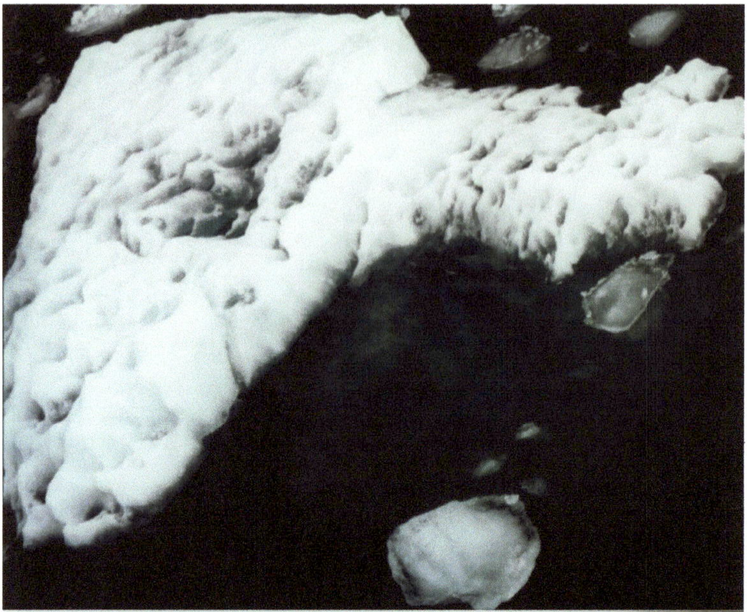

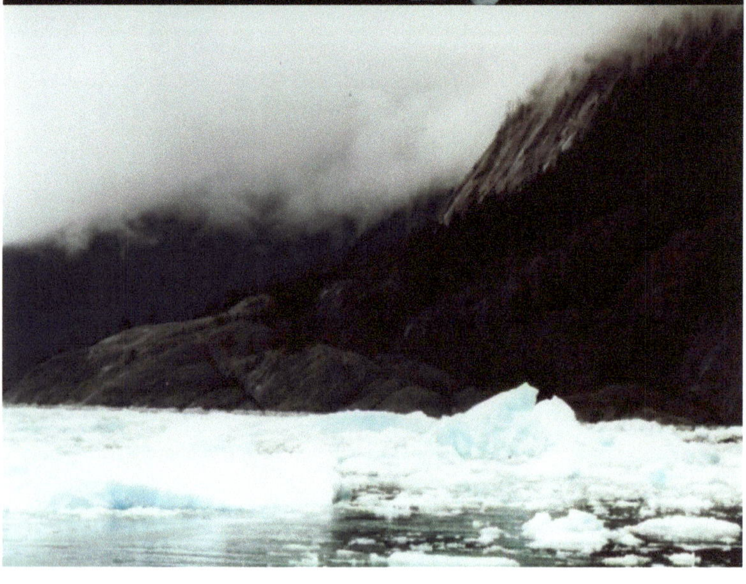

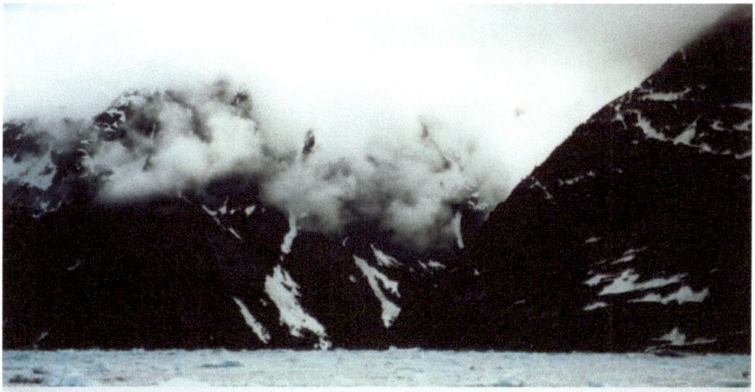

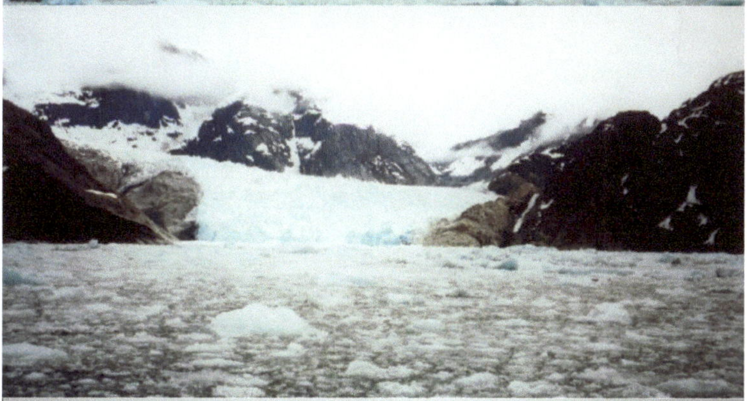

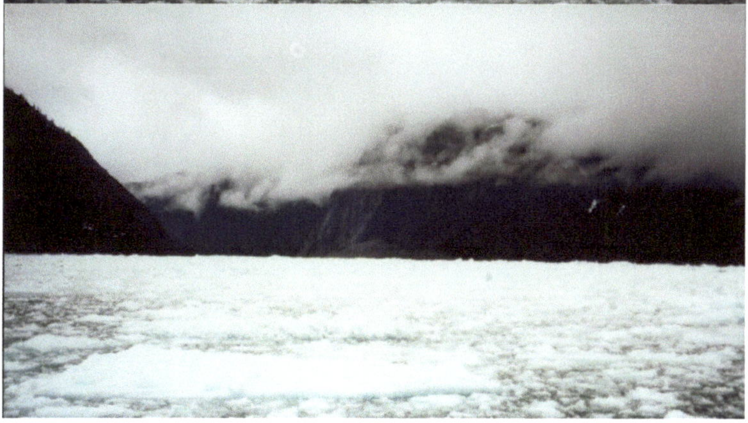

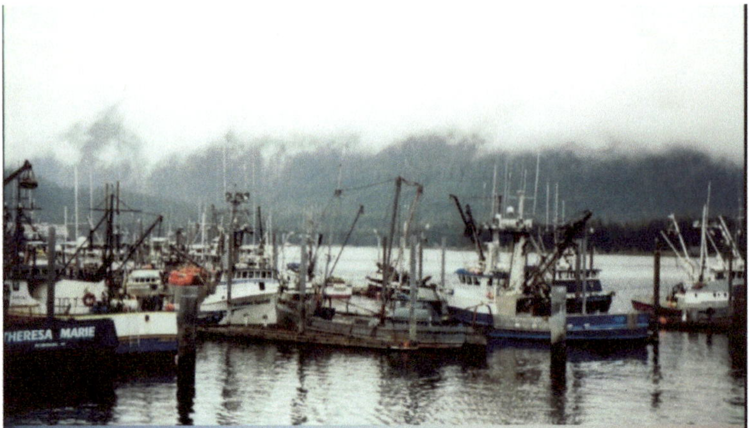
THERESA MARIE

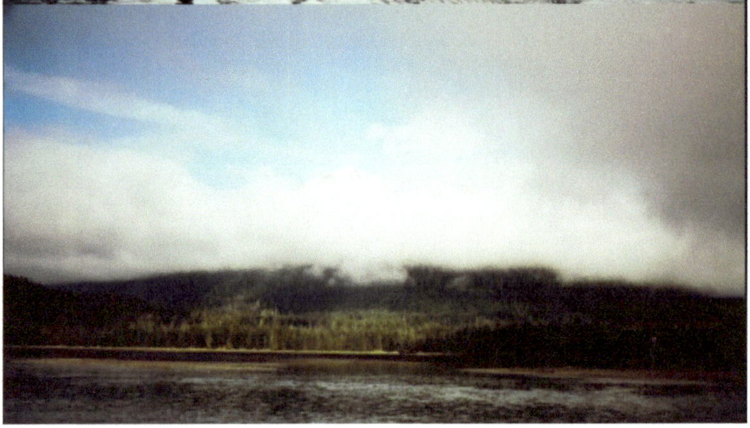

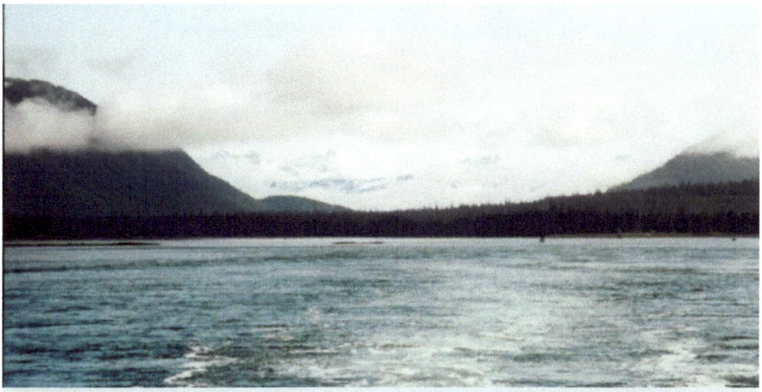

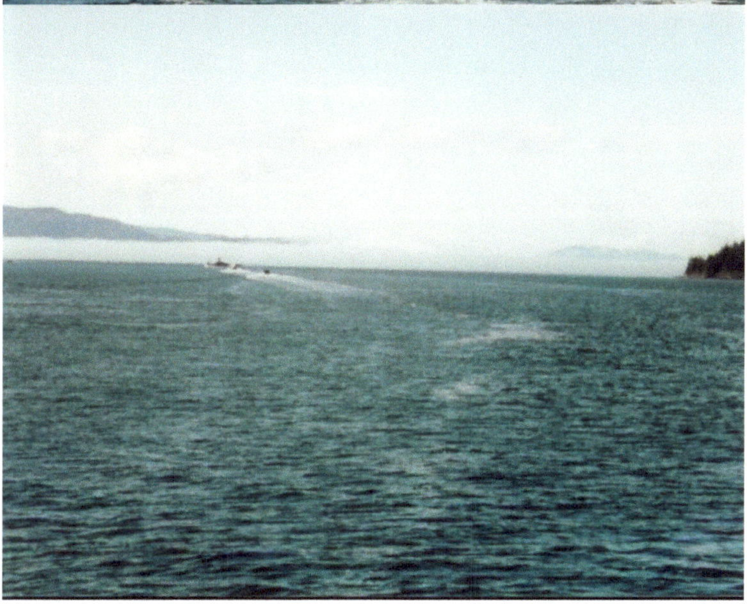

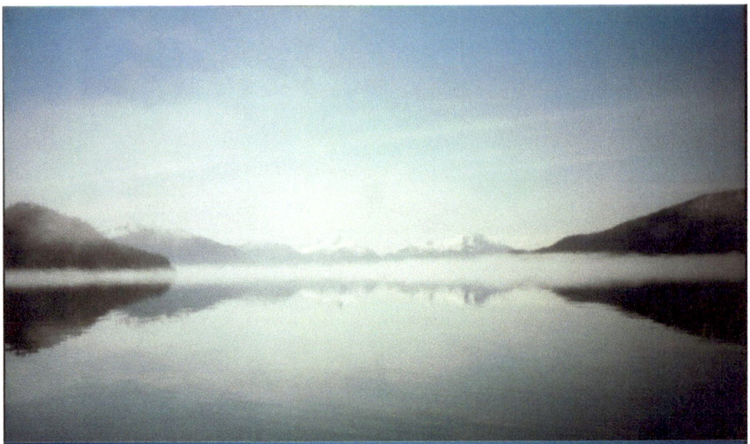
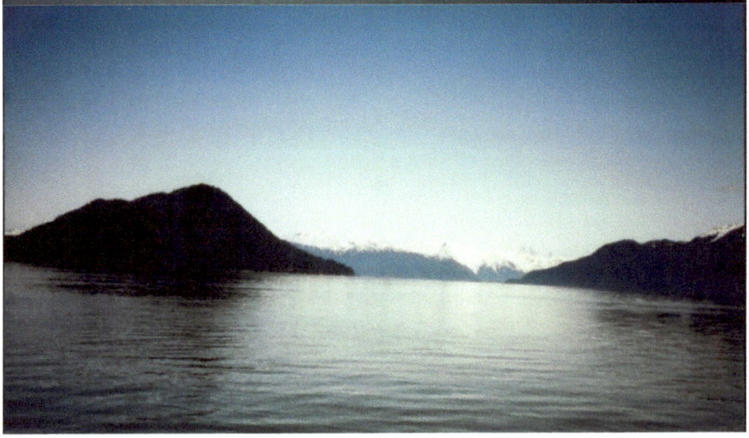

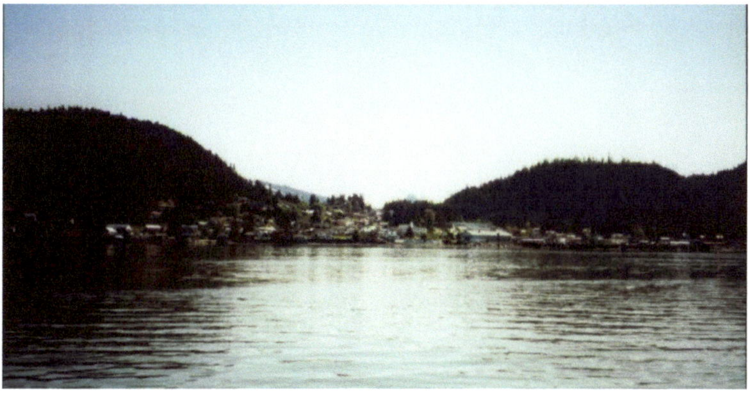

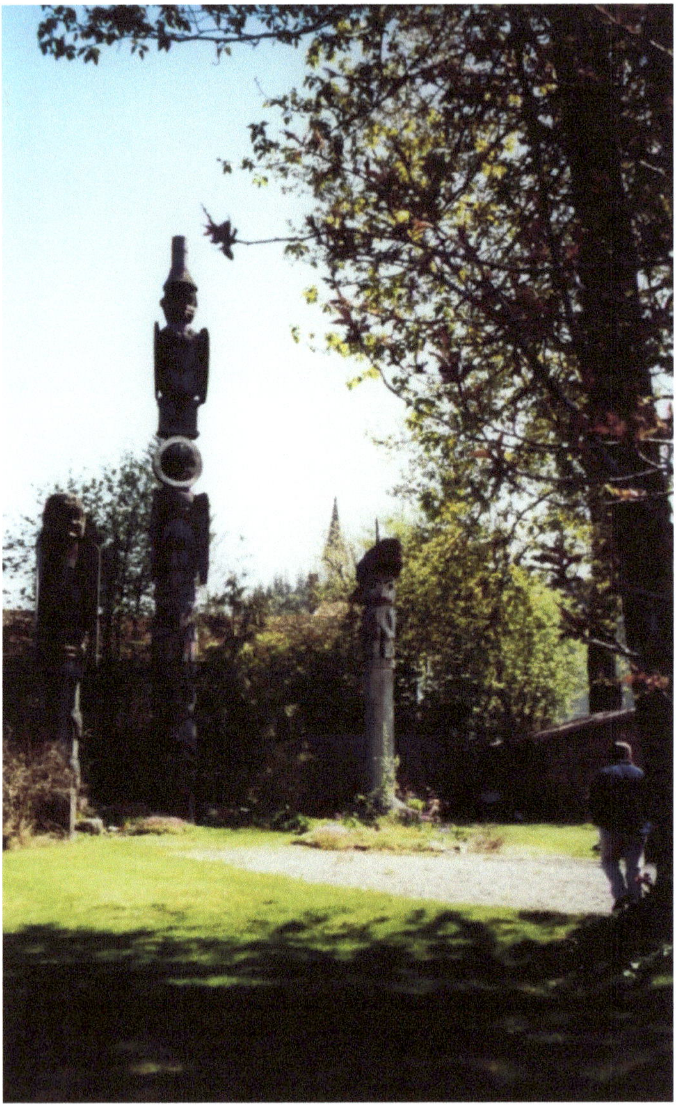

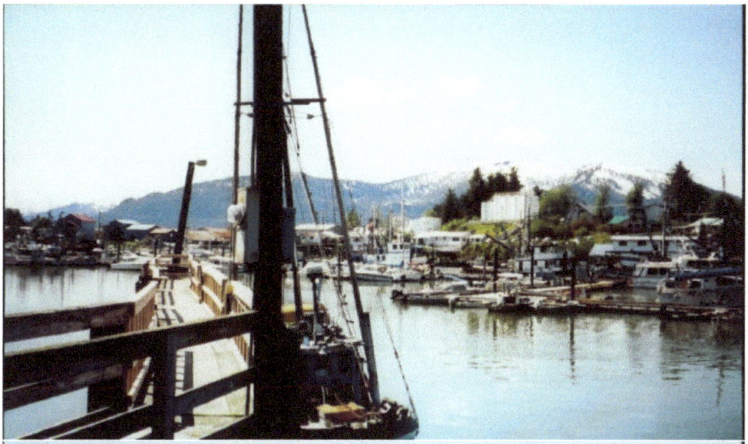

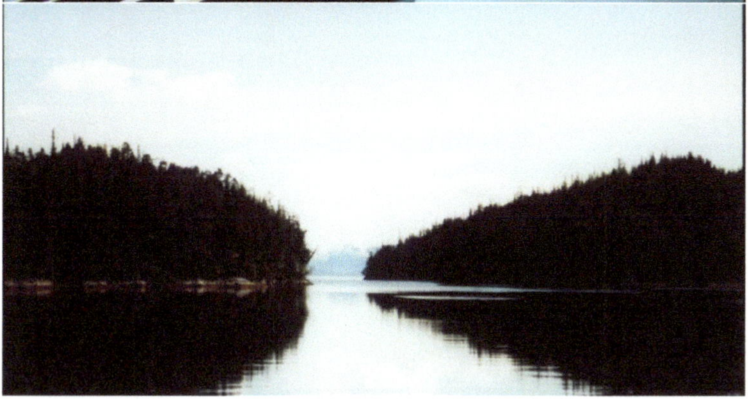

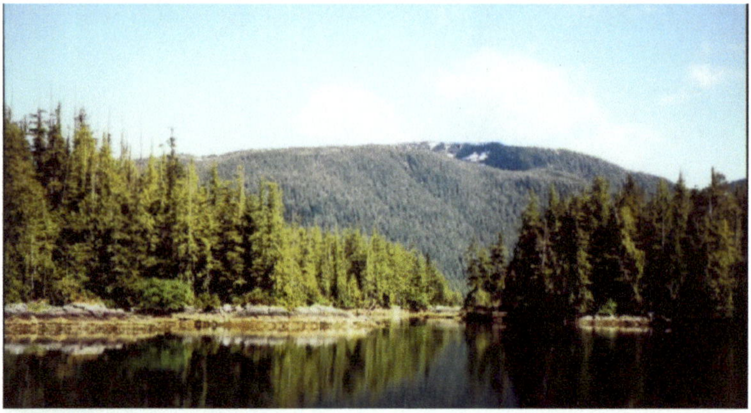

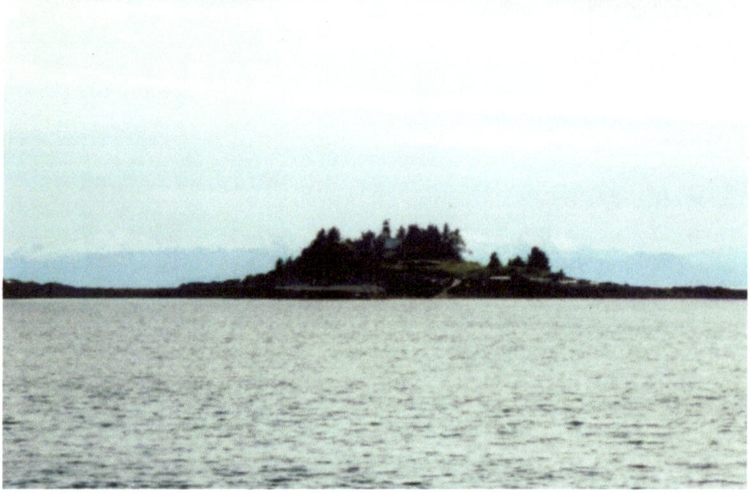

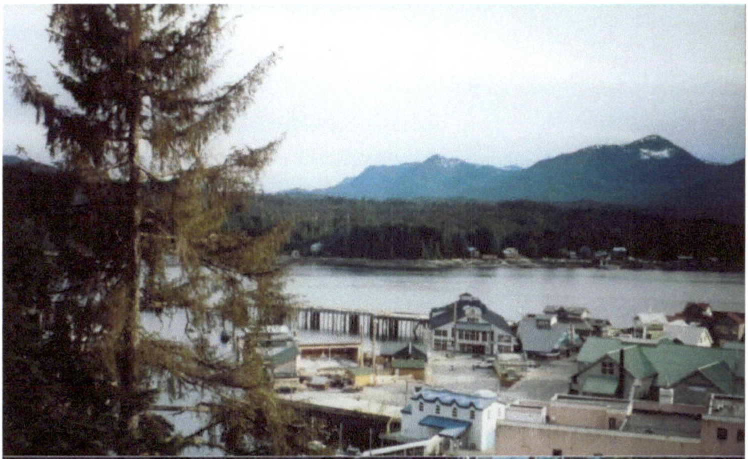

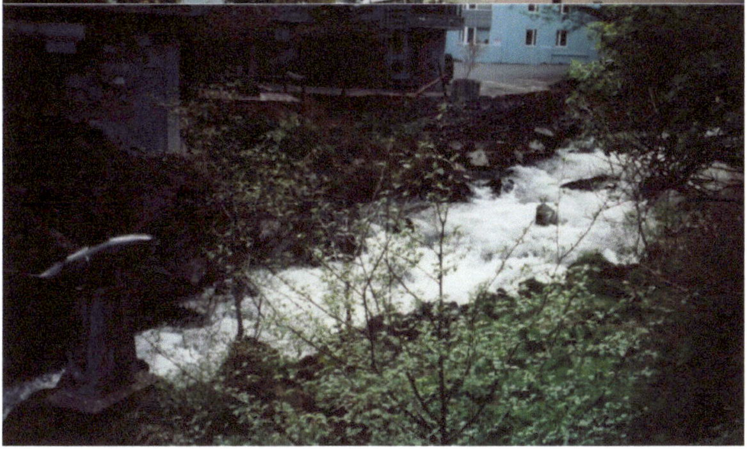

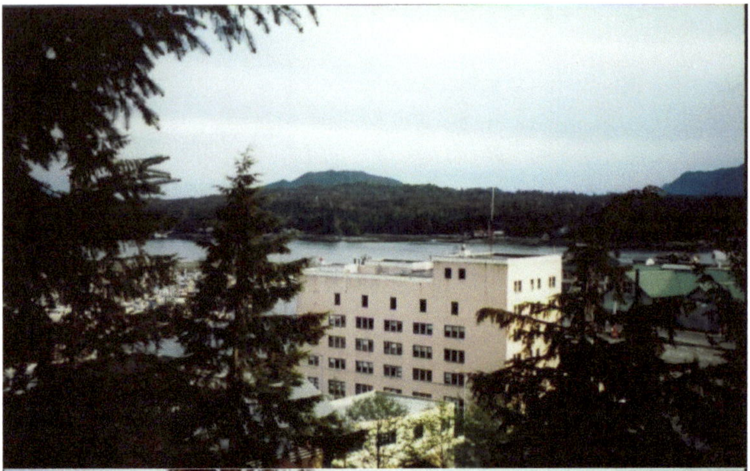

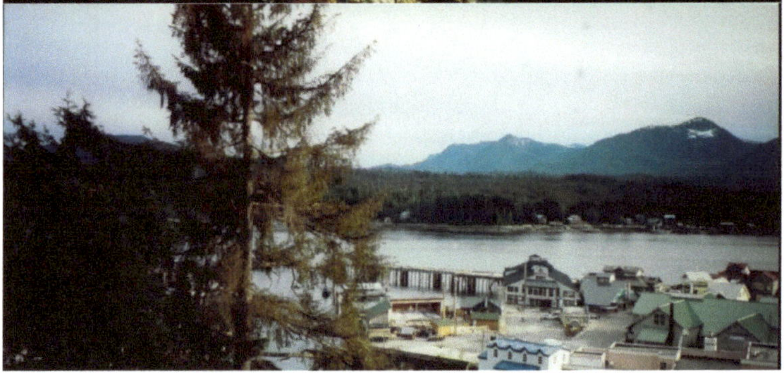

www.ingramcontent.com/pod-product-compliance
Lightning Source LLC
Chambersburg PA
CBHW040841180526
45159CB00001B/270
9781514339695